Acclaim for *Pursuing*

MW01227065

Pursuing Growth is an ide̲ ̲ ̲ ̲ ̲ ̲ ̲ ̲ ̲ ̲ ̲ ̲ ̲ ̲ ̲ ̲ ̲ ̲ ̲ entrepreneurs and business owners. Brent Banda provides a nuanced study of what it takes to grow your business and of many of the hurdles you will face along the way. He asks thought-provoking questions and gets you to consider all aspects of your business — from your business model to sales.

– Jeremy Miller,
Bestselling author of *Sticky Branding*

If you are an entrepreneur or small business owner, this is the type of blocking and tackling information you need to stay on top of customer needs and demands.

– Joe Pulizzi,
Founder, Content Marketing Institute; author, *Content Inc.: How Entrepreneurs Use Content to Build Massive Audiences and Create Radically Successful Businesses*

Pursuing Growth is a business owner's secret weapon for unleashing managerial talent in pursuit of growth, profits and organizational success. It is a book that reminds us that the answers to our most confounding business challenges are always in the room.

– Thomas William Deans,
Author, *Every Family's Business: 12 Common Sense Questions to Protect Your Wealth and Willing Wisdom: 7 Questions Successful Families Ask*

If you are thinking about growing your business by shifting direction, you and your leadership team need to read this book. It is the perfect antidote to the linear thinking we all develop after years of working in our companies. Brent Banda broadens the mind with the exhaustive list of where and how to mine opportunities in your company and your market – all with the customer in crystal-clear focus.

– Tom Redl,
President, Chandos Construction

Brent Banda's *Pursuing Growth* is a must read for the business owner on the go. It is the book you want to leave on your desk to have at arm's reach at all times. It provides a refreshing read on all the topics relevant to any organization that values its customers and success. I walked away refreshed with Brent's perspective on sales management, branding and social media.

– Sean Lavin,
Business Development Manager, Aircom Instrumentation

Pursuing Growth is exactly the type of book that I like. It's easy to read and has plenty of real-world examples that do a great job of communicating concepts and issues. On many topics I found the information that I needed and Brent's writing was educational, thought provoking and a great help for me.

– Patrick Richards,
Former Owner, Fisher Implement Company

PURSUING
GROWTH

PURSUING
GROWTH

Practical Marketing Tips
for Business Owners

BRENT BANDA

Steve,
Its great to see
the positive changes you
are making with the
Saskatoon Blades — good luck
building the business!

Brent

Sept 16 2015

MILE (84) PRESS

Mile 84 Press
Visit www.mile84.com

Library and Archives Canada Cataloguing in Publication
Banda, Brent, author
    Pursuing growth : practical marketing tips for business owners / Brent Banda.

Issued in print and electronic formats.
ISBN 978-0-9731369-1-3 (paperback).--ISBN 978-0-9731369-2-0 (epub).--ISBN 978-0-9731369-3-7 (mobi)

    1. Marketing. 2. Small business--Management. I. Title.
HF5415.B2837 2015   658.8   C2015-904600-9
C2015-904601-7

1 2 3 4 5 19 18 17 16 15

Printed and bound in Canada.

This book is dedicated to Chantal, Luke, Sophie, and Matthew. Thank you for your love and support.

Contents

Introduction: Insights That Drive Growth

In March 2010, I stepped carefully through freshly fallen snow and crossed the parking lot of a manufacturing facility. I was working with a well-established family business that produced industrial equipment. For months we had been developing a marketing and sales plan that would drive the company's international expansion.

The company had a strong management team. These people were smart. They knew their industry and their business. Today was decision day, and issues on the table ranged from the structure of the sales force to the brand image of a company the business had recently acquired. The team was ready to get to work.

Our conversation was intense. We took a deep dive into many of the issues and debated the pros and cons of various options. Strategy often requires difficult choices. There was no how-to manual for these decisions. They required a combination of good analysis and gut instinct. We relied on our past experiences, our knowledge of best practices, and the group's creativity.

The planning session on that cold March day went well. The business owner and his management team made good decisions. The strategy was sound and practical, and everyone was ready to focus on implementation.

Pursuing Growth was written as a support tool for situations like that – where business owners face difficult marketing and sales decisions. The book contains practical tips for growing your company. It's not written as a how-to book, but rather provides insight gained from my hands-on work as a consultant helping almost two hundred companies over the past two decades.

You will find that some of these tips will be relevant to your situation. Others will not. But chances are good there are a few gems in these pages you can use to increase revenue, volume, and your company's profitability. Take what is relevant to your business and run with it.

*Change is the law of life. And
those who look only to the past or
present are certain to miss the future.*
John F. Kennedy

A Vision for Growth

Growing a business requires us to be truthful and honest about the company's capabilities, competitive situation, and options for the future. But it also requires an understanding of what is possible, what we hope to achieve, and how we will make it happen. Growth stems from a vision for the future and a clear plan to shape a new reality.

Should I Invest in My Business?

Highly successful entrepreneurs realize more opportunities exist than can be pursued. One of the most difficult roles of a business owner is choosing where to allocate time and money.

The Entrepreneur's Trap

Most business owners are slaves to their businesses. The businesses are monsters that consume the owner's time, cash, and focus. The personal satisfaction that comes with success far outweighs the failures and the whole situation becomes tremendously addictive. Life becomes centered on continuous improvement and expansion. At what point should you ask whether a particular business is worth the effort?

The most successful entrepreneurs are objective. They learn to apply energy and focus on the limited number of opportunities that have the highest potential for success. They also ensure their resources are aligned with their personal objectives.

See the Big Picture

Most people are too wrapped up with growing their existing business. They are making important frontline marketing decisions each day, such as preparing an advertising campaign or restructuring a sales force. A business owner must first deal with higher-level issues.

First, establish the direction of the company. Two types of decisions need to be made:

- **Corporate Strategy:** Select the type of business you want to be in.
- **Product Mix Strategy:** Identify the actual products and services you will offer – and their expectations for performance.

Corporate strategy requires you to honestly critique your situation. Based on this reality, you must select the types of customers you want to serve and the types of products and services you want to provide. As an example, let's assume your company is a general contractor in the construction industry. Based on industry trends, levels of competition, and your own competencies, is your current business attractive in the short and long term? Should you consider diversifying from commercial into residential construction? Have more radical alternatives presented themselves, such as launching a new business to work as one of your own trades?

Product mix strategy provides direction to the businesses you choose to be in. In our example, if you decide to get into residential construction, what are your expectations for revenue and profit? Marketing decisions will stem from this understanding. What specific customer segments will you serve, what nature of construction projects will you undertake, and how will you make it happen? These decisions emerge from goals you set for the business (such as market share or profitability) and from allocating capital and management time.

The Role of a Portfolio

Consider a personal financial investment portfolio of publicly traded stocks. The companies owned in the portfolio would each face different levels of risk inherent in their industries. Also, management teams running these companies could be aggressive and wish to pursue growth, or conservative and wish to preserve capital. Most investors select a mix of companies based on their personal objectives and tolerance for risk.

If you are in multiple lines of business (perhaps you own several businesses or have numerous products), this portfolio concept is relevant when developing your corporate strategy and product mix strategy.

For example, let's assume you manufacture three products. Product A enjoys a high degree of customer loyalty and generates substantial profit and cash flow. Product B is breaking even, but has potential for growth and requires a considerable sales and marketing investment. Product C has seen profits decline drastically after being displaced last year by a competitor's new technology and your employees are convinced an investment in research and development would restore market share. Your product mix strategy should define a role and level of support for each. What portion of cash generated from Product A should support Products B and C? What performance expectations and management plans do you have for each product? Before you become engrossed in day-to-day operations, address these decisions to ensure the long-term health of your business.

Should I Grow My Business?

You have three options. Grow, maintain, or retrench. Entrepreneurs are hardwired to grow. That is a problem for several reasons. First, a growth strategy might not fit with the owner's personal risk tolerance. An entrepreneur preparing to sell the business may be better off preserving cash and ensuring short-term profitability rather than undertaking new long-term investment.

Second, the company might not be in a position to grow. Perhaps this company operates in a declining industry or is simply not able to keep pace with technological innovations, or perhaps the management team does not have the skills to operate a larger and more complex operation. Each of these issues can be addressed in some way, but capital may be better directed to a different venture.

Ultimately, the decision to pursue growth is based on your company's situation and your own appetite for expansion.

How Do I Grow?

When the time is right to pursue growth, consider whether to expand into current or new markets. Expansion within current markets is a fairly safe strategy because management usually understands the needs of existing customers and how they buy. Three common strategies are increasing market penetration (i.e., refocusing the marketing effort to increase sales of existing products to existing customers), new product development (i.e., selling new products to existing customers), and vertical integration (i.e., expanding to compete with a supplier or customer).

Growth in new markets often involves more risk than growth in current markets because there is less familiarity with customers. Two common strategies are market development (i.e., finding new customers for your existing product) and diversification (i.e., launching new products for new customers).

Market and product strategy serves as the foundation for subsequent decisions in your marketing plan. The prices you charge, distribution channels you use, and promotional efforts you undertake stem directly from your strategy.

Clarity Makes Managing Easier

Strategic marketing is a customer-driven process of strategy development. Rather than just ramping up sales, its focus is on making business decisions throughout the organization with this customer perspective in mind. It provides a valuable reference point for daily decisions on issues as diverse as expanding manufacturing facilities, developing advertising campaigns, and negotiating sales force commissions.

Keep the customer's perspective in mind when developing your corporate strategy and product mix strategy. What is your goal for this business? What resources are you prepared to allocate?

The concepts in this article are general principles and will manifest differently in each situation. But the likelihood of superior performance increases once you take a step back from building the business and ask yourself what you are trying to achieve.

Increase Profitability Through Market Penetration

Market penetration is a growth strategy that involves selling more of your current products or services to your current target market. Although there is no radical change to the company's corporate strategy, growing your market penetration often provides a significant opportunity to increase both revenue and profit.

Understanding Risk and Growth

When most business owners consider how to grow they tend to think of new products to launch. This can be risky. For example, selling new products often involves a steep learning curve as companies become familiar with selling and servicing a new technology. In other cases you may need to procure, store, or distribute these new products differently from your current product line. If you sell services, you may find subtleties in the service delivery process that will make or break your success with this expansion.

Entering new markets may also involve a considerable level of risk. A market is an identifiable group of customers. Because you are selling to new customers you may have to develop an understanding of how their purchasing habits and motivations to buy are different from those of your current customers. This new market may require considerable changes to your marketing strategy, such as breaking into new distribution channels.

Selling more of your current products and services to your current target market – market penetration – is the least risky of growth strategies. You know your business. You know how your current customers buy, what motivates them, and how to sell your current product or services. You have the advantage of momentum that can serve as a foundation for adjustments to your current sales and marketing process. You have the staff, operational infrastructure, and facilities in place to serve this market. The challenge becomes making meaningful adjustments to how you run your business.

Understand the Value of Incremental Sales

Businesses grow in stages. Overhead is often increased with the expectation of future growth. As a result, most businesses have unused production capacity.

Any incremental sale will result in only the variable cost of one more unit produced. Therefore, a minor increase in volume provides a considerable contribution to margin and dramatically improves the profitability of your company.

Increasing Market Share

The focus of market penetration is usually to increase market share. This involves attracting your competitors' customers. Many business owners naturally begin to consider tactical actions that are directed at immediate sales. Price discounting is an obvious example that may provide a spike in demand for your product or service. But customers attracted by a low price during a sale are opportunistic and will rarely repurchase at the regular price. At best, you may clear out some undesirable inventory.

Sustainable gains in market share are more likely obtained through increasing the perceived value you offer relative to competitors. Achieving that may involve making adjustments to what you offer the customer in order to genuinely improve your value, or being more effective in how you communicate so your customers actually understand the relative benefits of your product.

Increasing Usage

As an alternative to increasing market share, a company can increase product usage. Small changes to the business will often directly increase the volume or frequency with which customers use a company's products and services.

Take time to consider how the customer uses the product or service – and the situations that hinder increased usage. There may be minor barriers you can address with something as simple as a revised delivery schedule. More complex solutions may be required, such as altering consumer perception of the intended use of your product or service. A computer retailer with a service department, for example, may promote the productivity benefits of regular maintenance rather than just fixing a broken computer.

Creating Barriers to Entry

It is crucial to understand how to leverage your company's strengths when considering strategic options.

For example, operating with the lowest variable costs in the industry is a strength that can be leveraged to help ramp up sales while establishing a barrier to entry. Many companies with superior technology or unique processes have lower variable costs than competitors and therefore higher gross margins per unit sold. Rather than lowering your price to gain market share, it may make sense to spend money on increased advertising or sales support. Your new customers will be more loyal than price-shoppers who would have responded to a lower price. With substantial market share and a prominent sales and marketing presence, your company may have established a barrier to entry to deter potential competitors.

Do Something Different

Although market penetration involves selling your existing product or service to existing customers, you still need to do something different to see any meaningful gains. Business as usual will provide the same results as you've had in the past. Growth will occur when you alter your strategy.

Be innovative when considering changes that are genuinely valuable to your customer. Some options to consider include the following:

- **Educate customers:** It may be valuable to launch a promotional campaign that informs customers of the features, benefits, or even just the availability of your product or service. Many times people are simply unaware of your product or service and how it is relevant to their situation.
- **Make it easy to buy:** You may be able to increase the customer's ability to buy through increasing access to credit.
- **Broaden distribution:** Convenience, such as making a product available in more locations or altering when your service is available, may be a catalyst for sales.
- **Generate referrals:** Your existing customers likely know other people in your current target market. It is possible to leverage your relationship with an existing customer to inspire referrals. Referrals materialize differently in each industry because the purchase process and motivating factors vary. As a simple example, consider a health club that offers its members an entry in a draw for a spa-weekend vacation for each referral.
- **Alter product usage:** A simple change to a product, such as packaging in smaller sizes for more convenient or novel uses, may inspire additional purchases.

The complexity of pursuing growth lies with the fact that each company is unique, and each industry requires a different set of considerations for strategies that are both practical and have a high likelihood of success. By thinking carefully and creatively about how to increase market share or product usage, you may be able to increase profit without substantially increasing risk.

Timing a Product Launch

When is the right time to begin selling a new product? Do you want to jump into the market right away or wait and learn from the mistakes of your competitors?

Like most decisions in business, there is no single correct answer. You'll have to make a judgment call. The following factors commonly have an impact when a product is launched.

Financial Resources

Marketing decisions need to be tied to the company's overall financial management. Do you have the cash to support your launch plan? An early launch often requires a slow burn of cash, because it takes many months or years for customers to adopt your product. You just have to wait it out. A late product launch usually means sales will ramp up more quickly, but you'll incur higher immediate launch costs related to a crowded marketplace. Both strategies can work, but timing of cash needs is different for each scenario.

Tolerance for Risk

Is your company willing to make mistakes? Some companies are not, and they hate dealing with the unknown. Large multinationals are notorious for this. Most of their new product concepts are poached from smaller, privately owned manufacturers. The concept is reworked and launched on a grand scale, usually with several revisions and improvements that genuinely appeal to a broader customer base. However, early-to-market companies with a great new idea can still generate profit quickly. They are just less certain that customers will want to buy their product.

Receptive Customers

Customers must be ready to buy your product. Are people aware that they have a problem? If not, you must first educate them on the fact that they have a problem to solve before you begin selling your solution. Customer education can require a long and expensive advertising campaign and a complex sales process. A later launch will avoid these up-front costs.

A Fragmented Market

When a new product is introduced into an industry, the market quickly becomes crowded with competitors and all are fighting for a foothold. It is difficult to enter a crowded market late because you're just another competitor in the pack.

Once the industry matures, the market is highly fragmented and no single company dominates. Consolidation will eventually occur as successful companies begin to buy competitors and poor performers drop from the market. The key is to either hold onto a niche or be the company with broad appeal that can become the recognized brand in the industry.

Learn from Mistakes Early

Companies that sell mature products in mature markets have worked out the kinks in their marketing strategy. For example, they know how price points affect customer demand, and based on their desired volume for next quarter they can set pricing appropriately. Because they are used to predictability, the same companies make mistakes when launching products and are forced to employ a new marketing strategy. A manufacturer may sell through a retailer that has no appeal to their target customer. Prices are often too high or too low. Product quality or value may not meet customer expectations. Multiple problems may emerge, and customers are easily confused.

Be ready to adapt your marketing strategy. The company that works out the kinks quickly is bound to offer the most desirable experience to their customer, and this product will eventually surge ahead of the competition. Being early to market will help you gain this experience quickly.

Broader Acceptance

How much time is required until the mass market is ready for your product? Most new products sell well into a small segment at first, but require broader acceptance for the product to be profitable. Customers are finicky. Your corporate profitability and entire launch effort may be derailed if a broader market is slow in adopting your new product or technology. A later launch is likely to lead more quickly into a broader market appeal.

Much of strategic marketing comes down to judgment. Timing a product launch is no different. You need a deep understanding of how customers will view your technology and how your competitors will approach the situation. But you also need a good understanding of your own capabilities and resources. Business is a chess match, and when making a move it is important to consider all the factors that can influence the outcome.

Continuing a Period of Growth

The interesting thing about growth is that it involves change. After a period of strong growth, the marketing strategy that helped you grow may not be appropriate to take you to the next level.

Consider What Has Changed

When a company grows, the operating environment around it often changes. For example, a growing economy will nearly always attract new competitors. New entrants may bring a higher-quality product to market or perhaps a more aggressive price. The sales and marketing strategy you used to this point was designed for a different competitive environment and may not account for the strengths of new competitors.

To continue growing, companies also have to consider different types of opportunities than they did in the past. Growth is challenging, and companies learn from experience. They become better at what they do. Your company will now be attracted to more complex opportunities. Also, as your company grows you may need larger opportunities to see any meaningful financial benefit.

What changes have occurred within your business as your company has grown? Companies often end up serving customers they did not intend to serve and offering products or services they did not intend to sell. Consider a scenario in which you accept an order from a customer in a different market. Rarely do companies make money the first time they do something, so it is possible your costs have increased as a result of processing the order or adjusting product features. If your sales rep takes the initiative to bring in a few more of these out-of-market customers, you may now be selling to a market you never intended to target and are not set up to serve efficiently.

The point is that the strategy that got you here may not be appropriate to take you forward. It's possibly the wrong tool for the job.

Foundational Decisions Must Fit Your Growth Plans

Foundational decisions are the major structural decisions in your marketing plan. An example is choosing your target market. After a period of growth, it is worthwhile revisiting major decisions in your marketing strategy to ensure they are relevant to your operating environment and future growth plans. The following are three common decisions in a marketing plan.

Which Markets Will You Serve?

Often, the market you serve is based on which customers are profitable and also where you can ensure a sustainable source of business. Consider this situation. In 2006 I was working with a company that had grown rapidly and was serving a far wider group of customers than in the past. The owner realized a large part of his revenue was from startup oil service companies that may not survive if the oil industry experienced a decline. We decided to reorganize the sales and marketing effort to focus on customers he felt would survive if a crash occurred. If your customer base looks different after a period of growth, you may need to consider refocusing on a certain segment of the market.

Is Price in Line with the Competitive Environment?

When companies choose a price, they essentially have three options. A premium price is higher than competitors' prices, a parity price is equal (essentially focusing the purchase decision on non-price factors), and a discount price is lower. New competitors in the market may have pushed prices up or down. Your prices may have been set with a parity strategy in mind, but new competitors may have shifted prices lower. You may now accidentally be charging a premium price. This may be a problem if the product or another aspect of your company's offering does not support a premium price.

Does Your Brand Tell the Right Story?

Your brand is your reputation. A brand strategy is how you intend to adjust your reputation in the market. Often, companies grow by entering new markets. If you are going to diversify into new markets, the message to past customers may need to be different from the message to new customers, simply because new customers do not have existing knowledge of your business.

Activities Must Support Foundational Decisions

Activities are processes used to run daily operations. An example is how your research and development department creates new products that your target market actually wants. When a company has experienced a period of growth, its collection of activities is often out of alignment with foundational decisions. Take a hard look at your activities to decide if you need to make changes. The following are three examples that illustrate the diversity of activities that could be examined.

Does R&D Make Marketable Products?

When a company is growing rapidly, usually the research and development department is given a mandate to "go make us something." At other times R&D may simply be ignored. The people running the department will need direction and support to produce a marketable product.

Are Your Staff Qualified?

Before the financial market crashed in 2008, many companies benefited from a strong economy and training took a back seat to production. When that particular period of growth ceased, many companies realized they needed to refocus on quality and how they manage skill development. And to be clear, activities such as training influence profitability. Better training will improve value to customers, and more efficient training reduces operating costs.

Do Price Discounts Help Generate Profitable Business?

During a period of rapid growth, a "grow at all costs" attitude may prevail and sales employees often push for price discounts to capture higher market share. In an environment of growth, it is easy to lose sight of the fact that a company's primary goal is profit rather than market share or even revenue. In some situations, discounts can be used appropriately to generate new and profitable business. But far too often the tool is used as a crutch, and it either attracts unprofitable new customers that have no intention of making subsequent purchases or it radically erodes the margin on existing sales. Worse yet, the discount program becomes an expectation in future transactions. Careful examination of the pricing methods used to drive historical growth can have a dramatic impact on future profitability.

Consider How Your Situation Has Changed

Many companies update their marketing and sales plans annually. But the stage following a period of growth is an ideal time to take a hard look at your foundational decisions and whether the activities in your company actually support what you are trying to achieve.

In preparing for battle I have always found that plans are useless, but planning is indispensable.

Dwight D. Eisenhower

Planning & Execution

The process of planning helps us think clearly about our situation. It forces us to articulate our goals and the approach we'll take to succeed. In the act of creating a plan we must explain our assumptions, consider new options, and temper our enthusiasm with a dose of practicality that comes with tying detail to vision. In short, better decisions are made and we are prepared to deal with the inevitable curve balls that are thrown our way once we move to execution.

Structuring for Success

Most people seem to buy into the concept that it is better to have a mediocre strategy that is well executed than a great plan with poor execution. True, any plan must be well executed to see favorable results. But success starts with the plan itself and it would be foolish to duct-tape a plan together for the sake of moving on to execution.

When a business hires me to help with strategic planning, that business has usually been wrestling with one or more of the following issues.

Appropriate Care and Attention

A strategic plan can take a number of forms and be developed through many different processes. But a fundamental step is analyzing the company's situation thoughtfully and carefully, considering practical options, and ultimately deciding on a course of action. It is inadequate to just write goals on a napkin in a coffee shop.

Industry and Company Factors

The nature of the industry and life cycle of the company will often dictate which strategies are practical to adopt. For example, if you have a software company that develops applications then it will be very difficult to predict the competitive environment and even consumer trends one year from now. Rather than forming a structured plan with minimal room for judgment calls during execution, it would be a better choice to simply create guidelines for actions throughout the year. You may have clear objectives and general strategies identified, but you will need flexibility to adjust your activities. In contrast, an automotive dealer can fairly accurately predict its competition and consumer demand in the next 12 months and would probably benefit from a highly coordinated series of activities throughout the year.

Flexibility is also beneficial to companies in startup mode or those entering a high-growth stage in their life cycle. Companies operating in a mature industry will have the luxury of a more predictable operating environment.

Your Management Style

The management style of the people who will execute the plan should dictate the nature of the plan and decisions made. For example, some business owners are inherently structured in their thinking and are more effective when following a precise and linear planning process with consideration for detail. Other managers perform better when working with a loose, fluid, and highly collaborative process that focuses on high-level decisions.

Avoid Complacency

Planning can be a time-consuming task. It can be tempting to run the previous year's plan with minor modifications. At certain times a "business as usual" strategy is entirely the right course of action, but make sure to consider a variety of other options.

Avoid complacency by focusing on opportunities and risks that stem from the intersection between the operating environment and your company's strengths. These opportunities and risks will evolve over time.

Set Appropriate Goals

A major decision in a strategic plan is establishing the goals that your organization wants to achieve. Goals that are inappropriate, meaning either too aggressive or not aggressive enough, can be troublesome when looking to motivate staff to implement the strategies. Ensure goals are challenging but attainable.

Understand Your Limitations

One of the key mistakes that can arise in the strategic planning process is not considering the internal resources required to execute the plan, such as employee time and skill set. Take, for example, a company looking to enter a new market. The company may decide to use its existing sales staff to penetrate this market. Do these salespeople have the skills and personal relationships necessary to properly serve this new market?

Seek Employee Buy-In

Often, for a strategic plan to be effective, employees must buy in to a new direction or initiative. In some cases, it is valuable to involve employees in the strategic planning process. That doesn't mean employees from all areas of the company must build a plan through consensus decision-making. Rather, involving selected employees with relevant perspectives can result in higher-quality work. It can also encourage a feeling of personal ownership of the plan throughout the entire organization, as frontline or mid-level employees often perceive that their own perspective is considered when their peers are involved in the process.

To effectively seek buy-in, the effort has to be genuine. Each organization is different so the form that this input takes can vary. At times it is helpful to hold employee focus groups. At other times, it is useful to use employees as a sounding board for initial working thoughts on possible changes within the business.

Keep Your Hands on the Wheel

Maintaining control can be a common problem for managers who value a collaborative process. Despite the benefits of engaging multiple people in the strategic planning process, the effort can go too far. There needs to be a line between providing input and making decisions. It is critical that you take a leadership role and make the best decisions for your business. Collaboration doesn't mean consensus.

Be Accountable

Business owners encounter problems when a plan is created and no one is in charge of implementation. When making decisions for the upcoming year, make sure to delegate tasks to specific people with clear expectations about completion dates.

Be Flexible

The planning process provides direction and helps to coordinate effort toward achieving clear business goals. However, some entrepreneurs become too wound up in the plan and cannot adjust as the operating environment evolves throughout the year. The plan should be a reference document that lives and breathes. It should be altered as the market changes and relevant information emerges. Maintaining a current plan will help you to make better decisions throughout the year.

Nearly all companies have their planning process hampered by at least one of the ten points just listed. Increase your chance of success by keeping them in mind when developing your strategic plan.

Fine-Tune Your Marketing Plan

When preparing your company's marketing plan, consider the four funda-mental questions below. They drive to the heart of your competitive situation and provide insight into the profitability of your business.

Where Does Our Profit Come From?

Take a close look at your business. Examine the customers you serve and the products you offer. Are certain customer segments more profitable than oth-ers? Are certain products you offer more profitable? Probably.

Examine the gross margin, not just top-line sales. It is fairly common for hidden costs to creep into transactions with a specific customer segment or product. For example, let's imagine your company must use an alternative ven-dor for shipping to rural customers that results in higher selling costs. If this added shipping reduces your gross margin from 40% to 35%, does it make sense to continue spending sales and marketing dollars on this segment? Per-haps. Other factors may influence the decision, such as the possibility of lower competition in smaller markets. But at the very least you need to acknowledge the lower profitability as you choose which segments you will target in the future.

Few companies truly understand where their profit is generated. Owners, managers, and frontline employees become engrossed in the day-to-day op-erations of their business. They are too busy serving existing customers to look up and ask, "Are we really making money with this?" Sometimes the answer is no.

The more you know about where profit is generated, the better you can ad-just your internal systems and processes to ensure you are serving customers profitably. And of course we can refocus the sales and marketing effort on more profitable customers or products.

Profit source is one of the first areas I explore when helping a company cre-ate a marketing plan. Chances are good that the lion's share of the company's profit is coming from a certain customer group. There could be many reasons for higher profit. Certain segments may make more frequent purchases over the course of a year or have a tendency to purchase higher-priced items. It may make sense to target unprofitable market segments that have long-term growth potential. But that should be a conscious investment decision rather than an oversight. Clearly, your marketing and sales effort will generate a higher return if you focus on growing more profitable areas of the business.

What Do Our Customers Want?

Have you asked your customers what they want from you? You might be surprised by what you hear. This type of research provides two highly valuable pieces of information:

- **A window into another person's perspective.** Customers you have worked with for years may use this opportunity to address sensitive issues. This feedback is often candid and extremely constructive.
- **Practical and relevant ideas for improvement.** Your customers can have a slightly different perspective and often see opportunity for improvements to systems and processes. Small changes can improve working relationships and improve performance.

Companies can easily become so focused on trying to deliver something unique that they lose sight of what customers really want. For example, imagine an insurance brokerage that is considering opening up a new location as a way to increase revenue. Convenience is important in this industry, but is the physical location of the business the leverage point for increasing sales? Perhaps other factors would have a greater impact on revenue, such as extending hours of operation or simply adding additional staff in the current facility to minimize wait times at the counter. In this situation, it may be useful to seek customer input before making a considerable financial investment in a new location.

Keep in mind that market research is no replacement for a leader's vision. Customer feedback is useful when dealing with incremental change, but customers rarely have the perspective required to conceptualize new products or processes that can have a game-changing impact on the industry. For this, you must rely on your own insight.

What Is Our Company's Reputation?

A company's brand image can be described as its reputation with people who could buy your product. What do your potential customers think of your company?

The first step in establishing your brand image is to achieve simple awareness. After that, your reputation begins to form. Do customers know your company exists? If so, do they know what you do? Do they know what sets you apart from competitors?

A brand is built over time as a result of many individual points of contact. Also, each potential customer's view is shaped by a unique combination of personal experiences with your company (e.g., previous purchases from your company), advertising, and word of mouth. It is important to make generalizations and break the entire market into individual segments of like-minded people. Each segment may have a different view of your company.

Your marketing strategy should be shaped by your customer's opinion of your business. Is your potential customer's view of your company different from the reputation you would like to have with them? If so, your marketing strategy will have an uphill battle. It's not easy to reshape customers' opinions but at times it is necessary. If your potential customer's view matches your desired reputation then your marketing effort will likely focus more on simply achieving greater exposure.

What Drives Sales?

Take a step back from your day-to-day operations and identify the few key factors that drive sales. Examine what motivates your customers and the process your customers follow when making a purchase decision. Usually, there are one or two subtleties that heavily influence whether the customer purchases from you or a competitor.

As an example, imagine a manufacturing company that is aware of an opportunity to supply equipment to a mine undergoing a production expansion. Mining companies and the engineering firms that often handle procurement for new construction or expansions have a structured procurement method that generally follows a competitive bid process. But in some cases, a handful of production and maintenance employees may have considerable influence on the choice of a vendor. The purchase decisions for some forms of equipment are actually made on the production floor if the production employees believe a certain vendor's involvement is integral to the facility's operation. In a case such as this, the marketing and sales strategy must involve direct contact with these "hidden" decision-makers.

When designing your marketing plan, the four simple questions we just explored provide deep insight into your business and can help identify the primary factors that determine its success.

Building off Failures

Failure will exist in any business. High-performing companies are prepared to manage setbacks and learn from mistakes as business and marketing plans are executed.

A professional sports team is a perfect example of this principle. Professional athletes learn to adjust their strategy throughout a game, and if they happen to lose they will accept failure, analyze their performance and move forward. Business people tend to ignore their failures and embrace only their successes. The company remains blissfully naive about what went wrong, and people in the organization will tend to make the same mistakes over and over again.

Costs and Benefits of Failure

Businesses are sure to encounter failure for two reasons. First, decisions must be made with imperfect information. Second, your company is a collection of individuals who are constantly learning from their mistakes.

There are two types of costs to failure. Direct out-of-pocket costs draw down the company's operating cash and reduce return on investment. Opportunity costs that involve lost potential revenue may be less obvious but many times are far more expensive.

As a business owner, accept the fact that your people will make both good and bad decisions. Failure has an upside, because these situations present genuine learning opportunities. But failure's downside is a setback in performance. Decide how you will work through these setbacks. Allow people to fail while minimizing costs incurred by the company and keeping options open if events do not materialize as expected.

Flexibility Is Your Friend

When you face an uncertain situation, keep your business or marketing plan flexible and allow for adjustments to broad strategies and individual tactics. Plans should incorporate only as much detail as is practical to implement. The key is to build a plan that is appropriate for your situation, and then create an environment in your organization that supports effective implementation. You must have the freedom to learn on the fly and adjust as the situation becomes clearer.

For example, test whether a new advertising method would work before committing to a long-term contract. If you find the promotion does not meet your expectations you are then able to examine the cause. This allows you to make adjustments until you are confident you have something that works, then commit a larger portion of your time and budget to it.

Note that a highly structured and detailed plan is valuable when you operate in a predictable industry during a period of relative economic stability. Risk of failure is low in this situation. Upfront detail work will allow you to simply execute the plan efficiently by not having to constantly adjust your strategy or tactics.

Core Principles Should Guide Adjustments

If you must adjust your business or marketing plan, make sure you retain a focus on what factors drive success in your organization. Allow your core principles to guide the many diverse decisions that emerge.

These principles will be different for each company. Basically they are the key success factors in the organization. These will be different for each company because each business faces a different situation. Three examples of core principles are explained below.

Maintaining Culture

It can be difficult to maintain your company's culture through a period of change. For example, staff hired when the company is in growth mode will have a different view of the company than those hired during a period of relative stability.

Maintaining Profitability

It is crucial to ensure your employees understand that a setback does not justify a sustained period during which the company experiences an operating loss. Maintaining profitability in tough times trains people to focus on financial health and builds a strong base for superior long-term performance.

Retaining Profitable Customers

Failures take many forms, and more serious situations can result in a loss of customers. How can we retain our most profitable customers during a difficult period when things are not going our way? It is crucial to adopt a long-term view for managing your client base through the inevitable cycles of business.

Force yourself to identify only a select few core principles, and let these guide all decisions. This process keeps you focused on what is important in the long term.

Collect Good Information

When a company is experiencing a period of success, managers are emboldened by strong revenues and have the courage to make difficult choices. When the company experiences a period of failure, people begin to second guess themselves. Managers are often risk-averse and can be paralyzed by indecision.

Decisions become hard because these managers often lack a proper understanding of the situation. The original strategy that failed was likely based on the manager's current information. When faced with uncertainty, the first priority should be to learn about the situation. Educated guesses can be valuable. Frontline employees and department managers will see trends emerging and understand points of value that are important to customers. Trust the instincts of these frontline employees. Build on these industry insights in order to test-market new products or attempt adjustments to internal processes.

Monitor Success

Two months into the rollout of a plan, how will you know if your strategies and tactics are unfolding as you intended? What formal and informal systems are in place to gather necessary information? Do you know what results you are looking for before the plan is executed?

A good performance measurement program will provide valuable feedback on areas of the plan you can actually adjust during implementation. The program should also provide useful perspectives for building a future year's plan.

Focus on Execution

When your sales manager reports to you that a certain product launch has not met revenue expectations, does your company encourage that manager to make adjustments? Corporate culture is the atmosphere in the company that influences employee attitude and actions. Your company's corporate culture must create a supportive environment to learn from inevitable failures.

It is crucial to ensure the people executing the plan's strategies have a solid understanding of why those strategies are in place and how they are expected to unfold. When people on the front line understand the bigger picture, they are more likely to embrace the plan and also provide meaningful input when adjustments are required.

People who are used to winning often have a hard time accepting failure. People need to expect that some failure will occur. Back to our sports analogy: professional sports teams know they cannot win every game. The key is to understand why you won or lost and how you can improve.

A plan can be structured in a way that builds on both successes and failures. Often this involves managing your company's risk in uncertain times. You must also create an environment that nurtures employees' ability to learn from mistakes and adjust as information becomes available.

Someone's sitting in the shade today because someone planted a tree a long time ago.

Warren Buffett

Choices That Affect Profit

Choices dictate our lives. We can turn left. Or right. Or stay still. As business owners, our prosperity in the future is a direct result of the actions we take today.

Driving Profit Through Relationship Marketing

Relationship marketing is a simple concept. It focuses on building a continued relationship with your customer rather than completing a single transaction.

Some Customers Are Partners

In the 1990s, relationship marketing became the new buzzword in the industry. It called into question the value of short-term, sales-oriented marketing promotions and made people view customers as partners.

It can be difficult to treat all customers as you would a partner in your business. Be selective, and focus on the situations where there is a business case to adopt this partnership perspective. The key is to evaluate the customer over the long term. Instead of looking at sales volume in a region or market share in a market, examine the total gross profit your company can generate over the life of a customer relationship. Your organization is forced to make decisions such as

- Selecting your profitable customers and avoiding unprofitable customers
- Retaining your most profitable customers
- Gaining more of the total purchases your customers make
- Building additional value into products and services

Focus on Core Relationships

Relationship marketing has considerable benefits. For example, your business is far more likely to receive referrals from loyal customers who perceive your company as a business partner. Loyal customers also tend to be less price-sensitive. Naturally this philosophy of dealing with people will attract customers who appreciate a long-term relationship and are willing to pay a fair price for the added benefits of the partnership.

Businesses have always struggled with the concept of "the customer is always right." At what point does servicing a customer become unprofitable? Relationship marketing encourages an organization to consider the cost of customer satisfaction relative to the profit during the life of the account.

For example, let's assume your custom fabrication company generates $100,000 in gross margin annually from a key customer. That customer's procurement officer just informed you that a $300 part you delivered did not meet specifications. You have the drawings on file that prove your product met the customer's request exactly. The value of the relationship is obviously higher than the profit on this single part.

Rather than wading into a dispute, your organization must get the correct part to the customer quickly and ensure your relationship with the procurement officer is pristine. It would be valuable to ensure the procurement officer realizes the mistake did not happen in your shop, but you must also leave the impression that the customer can rely on you when a solution is required.

Adjust Your Business Practices

Ask yourself how your employees would have handled that key customer. Practically, relationship marketing is difficult to implement. It requires the organization to change how it does business and has implications deep into areas that are not normally connected to marketing. It focuses you on

- Placing as much emphasis on after-sale service as on the technical quality of the product
- Changing internal systems and processes to deliver more profitable work
- Sharing customer information widely throughout the organization, not just with the sales department
- Providing employees with authority to solve customer problems

Consider the difficulty of implementing relationship marketing throughout your company. It is crucial for all employees to understand why partnerships with customers are important. This system will live or die on the front lines. Everyone should own the customer, from the production floor to the finance department. We don't want our accounting department closing our best customer's credit account over a misunderstanding about an invoice.

As with most decisions related to marketing, good execution is crucial. Relationship marketing requires a cultural change within the organization. When implemented correctly, this customer-focused approach to building your business will result in a more stable and profitable organization.

Where Do I Spend My Marketing Budget?

As business owners, we often have too many great ideas about how to grow revenues. Should we invest our time and money this year in sales force training, a new product brochure, or radio ads? Marketing, after all, is more than just advertising and there are multiple demands on limited resources.

Rather than trying to decide between two diverse options such as a billboard campaign or a new website, take a different perspective. Start by focusing on customers that have an existing relationship with your company and determine what is required to encourage them to purchase. The first step is to categorize potential customers into four groups: current customers, former customers, potential customers we know, and potential customers we don't know.

Current Customers

An old sales force truism is to spend most of your time on people who are ready to buy. It is often valuable to invest your time and money with current customers because your effort is more likely to have an immediate impact on sales.

Your marketing effort with current customers can have multiple goals, including to lower the risk of a customer leaving, increase the number of transactions per customer, or increase the profitability of that account. You usually don't have to spend a lot of money on current customers, but you do need to put careful thought into how best to influence the relationship. For example, imagine a small-engine repair business that services lawn mowers each spring. The issue facing this business may be to retain customers. The solution may be simply to mail these current customers a letter encouraging them to book early in the season to avoid delays. You don't even have to offer a price discount.

The definition of a current customer will be different for each company. Current customers for a retail furniture store could be interpreted as people currently in your showroom. Marketing resources should be focused on areas such as the showroom experience (e.g., merchandising, ensuring adequate inventory is displayed) or the sales process (e.g., salesperson training, brochures, and other sales support tools).

Current customers for a manufacturing company may refer to people who make regular monthly purchases. Here, your budget should be focused on managing the ongoing working relationship. Take them out for lunch and ask them how you can improve how you do business. If a customer uses multiple vendors, your budget may be well spent pursuing a greater portion of their business.

Former Customers

As with current customers, marketing to former customers can have a high return on investment. These people are often easier to engage in the sales process than others who do not yet know your company.

Many businesses ignore former customers. As business owners we tend to believe former customers are familiar with our products and services and are aware of everything we can provide. Clearly, this assumption can be wrong and a sales discussion can yield new opportunities.

There can be many reasons why former customers no longer buy from us. In some cases, the customer may not have required any additional products after our most recent sale. But with time, a new need may have emerged. Have we stayed in contact with that customer? Customer appreciation events are often a fantastic way to rebuild past relationships. In other cases, the customer may have already begun to do business with our competitors. It may be valuable to focus time and budget on rebuilding those relationships.

The marketing approach you take to pursue former customers will depend on your own situation. These strategies and tactics will be influenced by your industry, your competitive situation, and your own company strengths. The key is to determine whether or not it is important to change how you manage relationships with former customers. You may be leaving money on the table.

Potential Customers We Know

Most business owners are pretty good at realizing the importance of qualified leads. Improvements can often be made in how these leads are handled. The most dramatic impact on profitability can come with simply being organized. A surprisingly large number of owner-managed businesses rely on sticky notes to track sales leads. A Customer Relationship Management (CRM) system is a software application that serves as a database of potential customers and tracks the progress made toward closing a sale. For most businesses, the annual cost of this software can be less than $1,000 per salesperson. The investment often pays for itself quickly, simply because potential customers no longer fall through the cracks. There are several CRM software applications available.

We can influence potential customers we know in many ways. For companies that are attempting to inspire a first purchase with the intent to secure a longer-term customer, a special promotion that offers unique product or special pricing may be appropriate. Industrial and commercial companies often find success in altering the sales approach. This might include the use of team selling or approaching the customer with an entirely new potential working relationship, such as an inventory management program rather than transactional sales.

Potential Customers We Don't Know

This category has the lowest return on investment because these customers do not have a relationship with your business and they might not be in a position to buy. However, this is where most business owners spend their time and money. Two reasons are common. First, most business owners fool themselves into believing they just need more leads in the pipeline. The opposite is true. Investing time and money in tightening up your sales process will have more positive impact on your bottom line than getting more people into a loose system where potential customers slip through the cracks. The second reason is that it is easy to advertise on radio, on billboards, and in trade magazines. Too many people chose to promote their business through mass advertising simply because it is convenient.

Investing in this category is valuable in situations where current customers or contacts cannot meet revenue expectations, such as during a product launch, during an aggressive push to rapidly expand market share, or in an industry where purchases are extremely infrequent.

It can be possible to integrate several promotional options to draw these customers into your sales process. For example, if your customers require a great deal of background information during their purchase process you may be able to steer people to resources on your website through direct mail or radio advertisements. The key is to realize what motivates your customers and the process they follow when making purchase decisions.

There are always difficult questions to answer when choosing where to spend a marketing budget. Should we focus on long-term awareness or short-term sales? What will happen if we never pursue potential customers that we have not yet met? Ideally you would effectively market to all four of the customer categories in the next year. But with limited resources, it is often valuable to prioritize based on the greatest expected impact on revenue and profitability.

Push Versus Pull Marketing

Children's toys are fantastic examples of how consumer demand can dictate what products a retailer will stock and sell. Every year there is at least one must-have toy to purchase because of heavy advertising and public relations effort by manufacturers, directed at end users.

For example, in 1996 the unexpected popularity of a toy named Tickle Me Elmo allowed retailers (and consumers who resold the product) to increase prices drastically from the original retail price of $28.99 to a few hundred dollars. Some reports suggest that the toy fetched as much as $1,500.

Much of the incredible demand is widely attributed to recognition given to the product by a popular television show. Although the product's success was an extreme case in which pull marketing was used, most companies look at incorporating both push and pull marketing to build a sustainable marketing strategy.

When to Use Push Marketing

Push marketing sounds much more aggressive than it actually is. It creates a situation within the retail environment where the manufacturer and the retailer work together to promote one specific product model or entire product line. Essentially, the distribution channel "pushes" a product to consumers.

This strategy makes use of a company's sales force, trade promotion activities, and promotional relationships to create consumer demand for a product most often at the point of sale (e.g., sales incentives/spiffs, coupons or discounts, and heavy product training for retail staff).

With a push strategy, the manufacturer works closely with distributors and retailers to determine how promotions will be run in retail locations and the expected volumes of sales that will result.

Manufacturers often look at incorporating a push strategy into their overall marketing efforts when

- Consumers do not know the product's brand or benefits, nor do they know how to use it and therefore need to be educated
- Consumers are price-sensitive
- The manufacturer is competing with an industry leader that has a large mass-marketing budget
- The goal is to inspire trial with the hope of building long-term product loyalty

When to Use Pull Marketing

Pull marketing creates a situation in which consumers knowingly request a branded product and "pull" it through the distribution channel. For this strategy to work, manufacturers must build consumer demand through heavy (and often expensive) advertising and promotional campaigns.

A pull strategy could arguably be more effective than a push strategy because it is easier to sell to a consumer who has a strong positive view of the product. However, creating this positive impression often requires a large amount of exposure over a long period of time.

Often manufacturers look to use media such as

- Mass advertising
- Word of mouth or buzz marketing
- Image advertising
- In-store advertising, sampling, demonstrations
- Viral marketing (getting decision-makers and influencers to become advocates)

Although this sounds easy, it often takes considerable time and resources to build awareness for a product to the point where consumers can identify it and request it in a retail environment. Often manufacturers will look at incorporating a pull strategy in these scenarios:

- Consumers want to purchase the product because of a strong affiliation to the brand.
- The manufacturer has created a product that is easily differentiated and identifiable from competing products.
- The manufacturer has adequate funds to support a large advertising campaign.

Each Situation Is Unique

Determining which strategy to use will depend on your situation and what you are trying to achieve. For instance, are you faced with the short-term challenge of moving a large amount of product quickly, or a long-term challenge of building sustainable demand and market share?

Push strategies are used to aggressively sell a product in the short term, and pull strategies are used to build strong long-term consumer demand. Businesses often use a combination of both.

When Teaching Trumps Selling

Potential customers may not understand their problem, their options, or how to even purchase the product. In situations such as these, a strategy based on educating your customers can be effective. Here's how it works.

The core of this strategy is focusing on helping improve the potential customer's knowledge of their options rather than promoting your own product. The point is to help customers become better informed, with the assumption they will be in a position to buy from you in the future. As well, this process assumes your product or company will be top of mind when they are ready to buy.

Three Scenarios

The strategy manifests differently in various situations. The following are three examples.

New Technology

Essentially, you have to sell the product category (e.g., soap) before you can sell your own product (e.g., Ivory brand soap). Consider a company selling zero-emission fuel cell–powered lift trucks to industrial customers that operate this equipment in high-throughput distribution center and warehouse environments as a replacement for traditional battery-powered vehicles. Usually, a company would approach the marketing process by stating its features that are relevant to a specific target market and by differentiating itself from competitors. The problem is that many industrial customers have no understanding of fuel cell–powered equipment because this technology is not yet widely used. They don't know the advantages and disadvantages compared with traditional battery technology or the factors that affect ownership, such as the maintenance involved. That means it will be important to explain the basics before you walk in the door trying to explain why your company's product is superior to competitors' products.

Customer Lacks Experience

Lack of customer experience can be a barrier. For example, a business may be a potential customer for a GPS tracking system that can help manage its fleet of vehicles. Chances are good that senior people in the company are aware of areas in the business that could be improved (lower costs, improved employee safety, greater employee efficiency), but the company will likely not have the experience with such a fleet-wide information system to accurately understand the specific benefits or costs involved by adopting this unfamiliar technology.

Technical or Complex Product

Potential customers may be fairly well informed about their situation and the product's fit but the solution provider is more knowledgeable about the technology and its application. The company selling its product must first provide some background education on the technology. This type of situation emerges in areas as diverse as information technology and custom-engineered industrial equipment.

Designing Your Marketing Program

If your company can use an education-based marketing campaign, the following are a few characteristics to consider as you design your marketing program.

Where Might Customers Need Help?

Identify the steps in the purchase process. If customers need information earlier in their process, you can tailor your information to more basic questions around understanding the technology. For example, many companies avoid focusing early in the customer's buying process because doing so usually requires a long-term investment in a potential customer. But this long-term approach can build strong relationships, and in fact may be necessary given the buying cycles of certain customers.

Returning to a previous example, the potential customer considering innovative fuel cell technology would likely be unable to switch from its current fleet of lift trucks after a first sales meeting. It would probably require meetings and approvals at many levels in the business. The sales process will need to focus on informing decision-makers and encouraging the inclusion of a budget line item specifically for this new product. This long-term approach is not for the faint of heart. With larger and more structured organizations the procurement process may naturally require bids from multiple vendors. So even if you are successful at having the product approved you may not necessarily be selected to supply it.

Promote the Category or the Product

To continue with our fuel cell–powered lift truck example, potential customers will likely need to hear about the core benefits of the product category (e.g., the inherent benefit of fuel cell technology for cost and performance) rather than the specific advantages your company offers over competitors. Usually, the conversation shifts to promoting your own product later in the buying cycle. But to start, the potential customer will actually be turned off if you are "selling" your product rather than helping them to understand a technology that will benefit them in a meaningful way.

Consider Sales Force and Distribution Structures

In many situations, potential customers will need one-on-one time with a human being. How will you structure your business model to provide the human contact that customers require? There is no one-size-fits-all strategy here. If your potential customers are not interested in learning about new technology, you may choose to sell through local vendors who have existing relationships in their home markets. If your technology is extremely complex and a dealer network will have a difficult time educating potential customers, you may wish to use your in-house salespeople. Each situation is unique, and these are only two dimensions to look at.

Provide Automated Information

Nearly all customers are comfortable researching a consumer or industrial purchase online for at least a portion of the information they require. When it comes to online resources, content is king. When done well, written articles and videos are highly effective methods of building credibility and positioning your company favorably with customers. However, keep in mind that in many situations there is a balance between human contact and self-driven research.

As an example, the process with which consumers buy vehicles has changed radically in the past ten years. Customers now do a tremendous amount of research before walking onto a car lot, which has dramatically altered the role of the salesperson in a dealership. But the salesperson is still the final point of contact with the dealership and has a fundamental role in closing the sale.

One common theme for an education-based marketing campaign is patience. Many entrepreneurs prefer investing in marketing efforts that provide immediate and tangible results. There is absolutely a place for tools such as direct mail and sales promotions. But savvy marketers have a well-equipped toolbox and understand there is always a right tool for the job. When your potential customers (or a certain segment of the market) require education it is valuable to listen and to respond accordingly. That usually means designing the marketing effort around a long buying cycle with considerable investment in providing information when needed.

Spend a lot of time talking to customers face to face. You'd be amazed how many companies don't listen to their customers.

Ross Perot

Your Customer

A marketing focus brings the customer's perspective to decisions made inside the company. Growth often stems from a deep knowledge of what the customer wants, how the customer buys, and how your company is relevant to the customer's situation. As business owners, we must encourage all our employees to embrace the customer's perspective.

Touch Your Customer

When you develop your marketing plan, focus on influencing points of contact that have the greatest impact on your customers. Most business owners simply don't take the time to consider when these crucial moments occur.

A touch point is any point of interaction your company has with a customer. These points of interaction are important because your business lives or dies on the health of its customer relationships, whether you own an engineering firm, a cabinet manufacturing facility, or an ice cream parlor.

Influencing your customer touch points will affect your business in two positive ways. First, it helps you move the customer closer to the sale. Second, it helps build loyalty that translates to repeat business and referrals.

When I prepare a marketing plan for a business, I examine the process people follow when they make a purchase. This involves identifying steps that are important to customers and the motivation behind their actions. In the world of marketing, this is called consumer behavior. Its study uses principles of psychology to understand why people make decisions.

As a simple example, consider how a business buys new office furniture. Let's assume that an office manager will handle the purchase. The key steps in the selling process are some obvious touch points, such as the initial phone inquiry to the furniture retailer, a meeting with the salesperson, a review of the quote, and signing the contract to purchase.

Look at this situation through the customer's eyes. Healthy relationships are built upon small actions. The salesperson must also consider points of contact that may not be as pivotal as delivering a quote, but will influence the office manager's comfort with the purchase.

Here are three touch points that are often overlooked and relate to this example.

Use of Customer References

Many businesses use past customers as references in their sales process. What response would the office manager receive when calling one of your past customers? If a past customer has been too frequently contacted for a reference, it's possible that person may not describe your business favorably. Use testimonials sparingly and only when appropriate.

Managing Delivery

The contract may be signed, but the furniture still has to be ordered from the manufacturer and delivered. Any contact with the customer after the contract is signed is still a touch point. If you find out the order will arrive a week later than promised, call the customer as soon as possible. You may have bad news but the purpose of your call is to keep the customer in the loop. People obviously appreciate the contact.

Sloppy Billing

Salespeople are notorious for sloppy billing. The deal may be done but the relationship is entering a fragile stage. Simply ensuring the charges are correct is not enough. To the customer, receiving a final bill is an important step in the purchase process. When they review the bill, the customer will check to ensure everything is in order. Build a level of comfort and confidence by clearly itemizing all charges and providing explanation where necessary. For example, if there was a $100 delivery fee don't just list the charge under an ambiguous description such as "Other Fees & Charges."

Marketing is more than advertising. A proper marketing plan involves strategic decisions and is comprehensive in nature. It involves adjusting your internal processes to influence the customer experience before, during, and after a sale.

The key is to keep your eye on the ball and make good decisions. Understand the points where you have influence over your customer's experience with your company. Understand which of these points are important, and why. Build your entire marketing and sales effort around customer interaction.

Talk to Me: Customer Dialogue and Strategic Insights

Most companies I work with have been in business a few decades – several as long as 100 years. They know their industries and their customers well through years of experience. But true insight into opportunities and challenges in their industry is not revealed by day-to-day operations. It emerges only when a company takes the initiative to understand its industry and its own company much more deeply.

Good strategic decisions stem from good information about a company and its operating environment. Be open-minded about where you get information. Sure, a company's management and staff are an exceptional resource and should provide the majority of the insight that drives strategy. But there is tremendous benefit to listening to what customers have to say.

What Are the Benefits?

I was recently working with one company that manufactures equipment for mines. It was launching a product that incorporated a new technology into a traditional equipment design. The global mining industry was expecting this technology to be adopted at some point because it offers considerable advantages for employee health and safety. When we met with one mine's employees who would use the equipment, it became clear that this new product was designed in a way that reduced operating cost of the equipment by roughly 80%.

Gems of information like this provide the clay we can sculpt as we design a marketing strategy for a company. My client knew the equipment's operating costs would be lower, but did not realize the scope of cost reduction involved or the dramatic impact it would have on the mine's equipment operating budget. Personal conversations draw out valuable information. Strategic insights are the primary benefit of talking to customers.

What Information Can You Receive?

Discussions with customers often provide companies with a deep understanding of the psychology behind how their customers select a product or a company to buy from. Strategy can be designed around the factors that motivate people and the purchase process they follow when making a decision.

Most business owners know their industry well and understand emerging trends. However, it can be highly valuable to see the situation from the customer's point of view. For example, if there is a trend toward automation in the sales process, how do customers perceive the impact of such a change on their relationship with your company as a supplier? Are there considerations you should address when adjusting the sales process?

Another valuable piece of information often emerges when customers begin sharing their thoughts on what they don't like about the industry or how your specific company does business. In some situations, I have heard my clients' customers discuss points of frustration such as long lead times on shipments or a lack of customization options. Companies can often make small adjustments to their sales, production, or administration systems and processes to address these issues. Small changes can often be all that is required to win over a potential customer. In rare cases, insight from these points of frustration can even lead to developing an entirely new business model that may change how a company does business and help it stand out from competitors.

Finally, customers can provide highly valuable information on your company's reputation in the market. This reputation is your company's brand image. How do customers perceive your company relative to competitors? Do customers truly understand what makes your company unique in the marketplace? More importantly, do customers find that unique attribute valuable?

How Do You Collect the Information?

There are many ways to collect the information you need. Different methods of market research are appropriate in different situations. The following are some considerations before you get started.

You will have more success if you clearly identify what you need to find out before you begin. Focus on the information that you absolutely need to know in order to make strategic decisions.

Formal surveys certainly have their place, but when seeking deep insight I have found personal interviews to be highly valuable. Personal interviews that allow for discussion are far more effective at drawing out the root needs of a customer, as long as the person representing your company is skilled in managing the conversation. It is crucial to watch for cues in the customer's words, tone, and body language that may indicate you need to drill down deeper. It may be helpful to have an objective third party conduct the interview in order to ask difficult questions and draw out sensitive information that people naturally have difficulty sharing when they have an existing relationship with the person holding the interview.

As an example, just asking someone to rank whether your company has a positive reputation from 1 to 10 is not particularly useful. Ask, "What are we known for? What rumors have you heard about our company?" Then the follow-up discussion unfolds. A skilled interviewer will dig deep into the comment to understand the situation.

Focus groups are similar to personal interviews, but it can be difficult to manage risks such as groupthink. This is particularly true if one customer in the group dominates the conversation. Also, if your company sells to other businesses rather than consumers, in many situations your customers may not want to share sensitive information in a group situation if their competitors are also part of the focus group.

It is also important to understand the limitations of personal interviews. For example, it is usually practical to interview only a handful of customers, and we cannot expect this group to represent a statistically significant sample of the larger market. Therefore, the sample should not be random. The goal should be to carefully select specific people with perspectives that are directly relevant to the questions being asked.

We want to know how customers perceive our company relative to competitors but any one of our interview subjects will be able to speak only to his or her own personal experiences. However, if we choose a person with decades of industry experience at multiple companies we may find that this perspective is fairly well rounded. We should not assume that it represents the entire market, but rather that it represents an informed and experienced customer in our market. To complement this point of view, we may also select someone we know to be dissatisfied with our company and who can provide a valuable point of view on areas in which our company can improve.

The bottom line is that good strategic decisions require an understanding of the operating environment and your own company. Supplement your own knowledge with additional perspectives such as those of key employees, peers in your industry, and of course your customers.

Cultivating Profitable Customers

An important step when effectively marketing your business is to understand your current customer base. There are many dimensions to examine, but one of the most insightful is identifying the most profitable segments you serve and estimating the lifetime value of each segment.

With this information, small and medium-sized companies can plan how to focus their time and marketing budget to attract and increase business with customers in their highly profitable segments.

Not All Customers Are Equal

Some customers are more valuable than others. Before you spend a dollar of your marketing budget or an hour of your sales time, consider which customers are driving your company's profitability.

First, segment your current customer base into groups based on characteristics that are relevant to the sale. Keep in mind that a customer will not be part of two different segments. There are many different ways to group customers, and how you choose to segment the market is entirely up to you (e.g., demographics, psychographics, geographic location). The important thing is that there be some meaningful difference in how or why each segment buys from you. Different segments should purchase products for different reasons or through different processes.

Next, calculate the lifetime value of each segment's average customer. Lifetime value is the total sales revenue for a customer over the life of the relationship minus the costs associated with the sale (e.g., cost of goods sold, sales commissions). Essentially this is the profit per sale multiplied by the number of sales in a customer's lifetime. In a relationship business, you may want to include the value of referrals in your estimate. The lifetime value will be different for each segment of your market, because factors such as profit margin and frequency of purchase vary by segment.

How much is each market segment currently worth to you? Simply multiply the lifetime value of an average customer in each segment by the number of customers you are currently serving in that segment. You can also calculate the potential value of each segment by multiplying the value of a segment's average customer by the number of customers you could potentially serve in that segment.

What have we learned? We have identified our profitable customer segments and the actual and potential value of each. Knowing this can help you determine whether to grow your business in a segment or get out of that segment altogether. Remember, this is only one piece of information, and when planning your strategy you must also consider other issues such as level of competition.

Gaining a Greater Share of Your Customer's Wallet

Once they have identified the more profitable segments, most small and medium companies begin planning how to attract new customers. Although this is important, also examine growing your business with your existing profitable customers.

What you really want is a greater share of the purchases these people make. Most companies never consider pursuing additional revenue from their current customers. This revenue is often the low-hanging fruit for many small and medium-sized businesses. Usually, smaller local companies have based their business on personal relationships with customers. Customers already know your business, trust you, and like doing business with you. But many times business owners are so busy running the business they don't see opportunities for incremental growth. Do your current customers spread their business around to a few suppliers? Can you sell complementary products to these customers? Can you increase the frequency or quantity of the purchases your customers make?

A simple method of building business with existing customers is to ensure they are aware of all that your company offers. Many small and medium-sized businesses do not properly communicate this to their customer base or their market. Increasing customer awareness can involve an education process, and the best way to send a clear message is often by presenting a situation to which your customer can relate. A promotional campaign that showcases a product or a customer testimonial is often quite effective. You have an existing relationship with these people. Use it to your advantage.

Many times the best way to identify revenue opportunities is to ask your customers for feedback. Ask them how many suppliers they use, why, and what they buy from each company. Ask them how they choose what to purchase, when, and how you could change your business to accommodate their situation. There are many ways to conduct this type of research, from formal focus groups to casual conversations with customers. Whatever process you use, seeking input from your customers will go a long way to understanding what they want from you.

Encouraging Referrals

Once you have increased sales to the people you currently serve, it is time to focus your energy on attracting new customers. Start by getting help from people who know your business. Encourage referrals by leveraging your existing relationships.

Three things must happen for you to get profitable referrals:
• People must understand what you do.
• People must know the type of customer best suited to your business.
• People must trust that you'll do a good job.

Part of the goal is to get appropriate referrals that can genuinely become profitable customers. It's your responsibility to inform potential referral sources about the product or service you offer and the type of customer you'd like to attract.

Regarding the need for potential referral sources to trust you'll do a good job, consider the following scenario. Someone asks you to refer a plumber. An old friend of yours is a plumber, but you know that his company is unreliable. Would you make the referral? When people refer your business they are putting their own reputation at risk. To encourage referrals, work to build your company's reputation with the people most likely to refer you to a potential customer. Do exceptional work for these potential referral sources and make sure to show that others in the community trust you by showcasing customer testimonials.

Whether they have large marketing budgets or not, all businesses must have a plan to get customers through the door. Focusing on the right customers can significantly improve profitability.

> *The way to a good reputation is to endeavor to be what you desire to appear.*
>
> Socrates

Your Brand

A company's reputation can be its most valuable asset. A customer's impression of a company and its products is often built over many interactions during an extended period of time. As business owners, we must first clearly define how we would like our companies and products to be perceived. All actions will stem from this basic understanding.

Building a Strong Brand

Branding is a term that all business owners come across but few truly understand. Branding in business is similar to branding on a ranch. You leave your mark on your customer's mind.

What Is a Brand?

A brand is a reputation. This reputation is often represented by a name, term, symbol, or special design (or some combination of these elements) that is intended to identify a company or its product. The most effective way to accurately describe the strength of a brand is by the feeling you get when you see or hear all components of the company's image truly represented within the brand. For example, McDonald's has established a strong brand identity by evoking feelings representative of a fun and cost-effective family dining experience. The phrases, "Two all-beef patties, special sauce, lettuce, cheese, pickles, onions on a sesame seed bun" and "I'm loving it!" have staying power because they invoke similar feelings of what McDonald's represents.

The company's personality can also be considered a brand. It is shaped by corporate culture and defines what a company stands for. This is essentially the company's internal brand. Often, the branding effort starts internally because employee contact with customers greatly defines a company's external reputation. When developing marketing strategy, external and internal brands are inseparable and we must view them as two sides of the same coin.

Purpose of Branding

A strong brand identity is an effective way to stand out from competitors. If you do your job right, potential customers will know what you have to offer and think of you when the time comes to make a purchase. Your product's name may even become universally used. Take Kleenex as an example. The actual term for the product category is facial tissue, but nearly everyone refers to facial tissue by the most popular brand name on the market.

A successful brand can provide benefits such as enhanced brand loyalty or an ability to charge a price premium. Owner-managed companies often find that they have built a strong following of customers who receive tremendous value from a company they have come to trust.

Defining Your Brand

Branding is the action of portraying the image you believe will attract your target market. When defining what your brand should be, consider why your customers purchase from you. Doing so is much more complex than it first appears. The trick is to clearly define what is important to your customers and then build your competitive advantage around meeting those needs more effectively than the competition does.

Once you have defined and established your competitive advantage, it should then be communicated through an appropriate message and tone and reinforced in all contact with the target market. For example, McDonald's communicates its fun family atmosphere and fast, affordable food in everything from advertisements and layout of the store to the company's pricing strategy.

How Do I Build a Strong Brand?

When branding a company, product, or service, consider all elements that will influence the customer's buying experience. Strategic marketing decisions such as the prices you set, your product attributes, and even where you choose to sell your products can have a direct impact on a customer's opinion.

Brands are built largely through personal experience rather than promotions, because customers tend to trust their own experiences more than advertising. Therefore, a significant component of your marketing strategy should relate to customer experience. You may be justified spending your marketing budget within your own company to help "live the brand."

There is no doubt that advertising often influences the formation of a brand, but it can also play a role in sustaining the brand over time. This type of advertising is usually broad, image-based advertising. Walmart, for example, advertises everyday low prices instead of weekly specials.

When making advertising decisions, carefully consider how people will view your company. Imagine if BMW were to show a 16-year-old driver with green hair and a nose ring in a TV ad. This would not fit with the image of a typical BMW owner and could cause current BMW owners some concern that their status symbol is in jeopardy. BMW targets high-income adults and must reinforce this with every experience their customers have with the company.

Although it can take years to successfully build a brand, it can be easily destroyed. If Walmart suddenly started to sell high-end premium-priced furniture, its loyal customers would become confused and perhaps think that everyday low prices may not apply to everything in the store. Strategic marketing decisions such as price and advertising message are almost always interconnected.

Know Your Customer

The more you know about your customers, the more effective you will be at making marketing decisions. Who are you trying to attract as a customer, and what is important to that person? These questions are fundamental to your marketing effort whether you are selling industrial equipment to Brazil or cutlery in a mall retail store.

Why do these people buy? What is motivating them to purchase? Once you know the few key factors that influence purchase decisions, you can build those traits into your brand.

Knowing why customers buy has implications for companies planning to target new segments. If you plan to attract a new type of customer, should you adjust your brand image to include traits that are important to the new market segment? Ideally, yes. But practically this may not be possible. Honda faced this problem when launching a line of luxury vehicles in North America. The Honda name was well respected as an economy car and likely would not be suitable in the luxury segment. The solution was to launch an entirely new brand under the name Acura. Most Acura owners realize they are driving a Honda product, but the fact it's an Acura adds some credibility to the vehicle as a luxury car.

Know What Is Important

Define what your brand should mean to the customer. Again, it seems like a simple step but few business owners have a clear understanding of what they want their customers to know about their company. A company or product's brand should emphasize a few key traits. Sure, you can emphasize many traits that might be valuable over time (e.g., quick delivery, competitive price, or great service) but a select few will truly differentiate you from the competition and will also be valuable to the customer.

Remember, different people view brands in different ways. Too often, marketers speak about their brand as if all customers in one market segment are clones. Every person walking down the street has been influenced in different ways. Some people have had good experiences with your company, and others have not. Some have seen your advertising and others have heard of your business only through word of mouth. Keep an open mind when trying to understand how the market views your brand.

Growth Through Brand Repositioning

Increased competition, pricing demands, and changing markets can affect a company's market share and bottom line. When faced with these situations, companies often turn to repositioning as a way to create new appeal for existing customers and embrace new growth opportunities.

Repositioning is the process of identifying and leveraging a company's key competencies to redefine its brand to be more competitive.

Determine a Strategy

The process of determining an appropriate growth strategy will require you to build on the foundation of your company's key competencies. These competencies will be rooted in strengths that are valuable to the customer and provide a point of differentiation from competitors. For example, your company may be the best in the industry at delivering on time and on budget.

Four Basic Approaches to Repositioning

The extent of a company's repositioning efforts will depend on the degree of change in customer tastes, lifestyle, and attitudes as well as influences from the competitive market. There are four basic approaches that an organization can take to reposition its brand:

- Change the image of the product, but keep the product and target market the same.
- Modify the product to make it more attractive to the current market.
- Promote the same product to a different customer segment.
- Alter both the product and the target market.

An Example

Since the 1950s, Cadbury Snack had been positioned as one of the leading confectionery brands in the United States. However, over the years its consumer loyalty ratings had dropped. Through research, the company identified that consumers perceived the Snack brand as being appropriate for an older, more established customer segment.

Wanting to appeal to a younger target market (ages 25–35), Cadbury refreshed its brand by updating the look of its packaging, displays, and marketing communications to portray a more cheerful and lively appearance. It also incorporated an advertising campaign that depicted the product being enjoyed in a work environment.

These revisions to Cadbury Snack's brand and target market proved to be successful, as the company increased its customer loyalty rating by 5% in 2005 over its rating in 2004.

As Cadbury Snack did, it is important for a company to set out realistic goals and steps for what it is trying to achieve with its new positioning strategy. Had Cadbury Snack revised its product into an athletic food bar instead of repositioning its original product's brand, its existing and potential customers may have become confused with how the product related to the Cadbury family of products that are perceived as sweet treats. This could have had a negative impact not only on Cadbury Snack but also on other Cadbury products.

Three Steps for Success

Three steps can help a company ensure success when repositioning its brand:

- Determine context for the degree of allowable change. Most customers have a specific definition of what the brand is and what it can be relative to their frame of reference. Repositioning a brand too far from this frame of reference creates customer confusion (rendering the repositioning unsuccessful).
- Create a bridge for customers to make a logical and emotional connection between their current brand perceptions and the intended one. If an association is made, then it is more likely that customers will extend the same feelings to the repositioned brand.
- Ensure that the company can consistently deliver on what it promises.

By properly implementing one of the above strategies, a company is often able to increase sales with existing customers while possibly attracting a new customer base.

Marketing and Being Unique

We are bombarded with images of brands that have built their success on a trait that consumers perceive as unique. For example, Volvo has been at the forefront of safety engineering since its inception and many consumers still believe Volvo is the safest vehicle available. This is the basis for differentiation as a marketing strategy. Offer something unique that your target market finds valuable.

Process of Differentiation

Differentiation involves offering a benefit that competitors don't offer. Usually this means the company will have a unique attribute or combination of attributes. For example, a company may have the most highly skilled employees in the industry, a novel product feature, or superior systems and processes.

Differentiation is more difficult than it sounds. First, it is extremely hard to be unique. The product or service life cycle seems to be shorter these days. Part of the reason is open access to information. For example, consumers often expect companies to post technical specifications of products online, where competitors can access that information. Also, consumers seem far more finicky than in the past. People simply want the newest and best right away. BlackBerry's downfall illustrates this. The company's global market share plummeted between 2008 and 2013 as it struggled to offer something unique and relevant to consumers.

Second, customers actually have to want the unique trait you are offering. Imagine the local automotive mechanic shop that invests heavily in a comfortable reception area and waiting room. The decor is modern and spacious. There are three large-screen televisions, a well-stocked juice fridge, and even an espresso machine. These features may differentiate the business from competitors, but few customers would pick a mechanic shop based on the reception area. Other traits are likely more desirable to most consumers, such as a convenient location or reputation for quality work.

When You Are Not Unique

How can companies that aren't unique survive in the marketplace? Many will not. But some have built their business on personal relationships and being good at what they do. Rather than offering something unique, they are best described as competent. Customers keep coming back because of a desire for consistency, familiarity, or loyalty – or just out of habit. It's a dangerous situation, because these companies are generally underperforming financially and do not have a strong competitive foothold in the marketplace. New competition or emerging technology can easily provide the straw that will break the camel's back.

If your company finds itself without a differentiated product, the obvious course of action is to develop an attribute or combination of attributes that allows it to provide something unique in the marketplace.

This is the essence of competitive advantage. Of course, it is also a long and difficult process. But it is necessary to ensure the long-term health of your organization.

Start by understanding your customers. What is important to them? What are their core motivations when making a purchase? What steps do they follow when collecting information and when they finally make the transaction?

Yes, these are basic questions, but business owners are so busy running daily operations that the questions are rarely asked. People are preoccupied with trying to close the next sale and get products shipped on time. Rarely will a company's management take a deep dive and truly understand their customer's buying behavior. When I work with clients, people almost always learn something about their customers that fundamentally changes strategic decisions.

Once you know what is important to customers, consider how those needs are being met. Are competitors in this marketplace, including your own company, currently providing what customers really want? This analysis will show you if any gaps exist in the market.

Can your company be better than competitors at providing what customers want? That's the difficult step. It will take time and money to develop an attribute that genuinely differentiates you from competitors, which is why it is important to focus on an area that is meaningful to the customer.

Considerations for Segmentation

The process of differentiating your company from the competition starts with the concept of segmentation. Different groups of customers want different things.

The key is to define segments based on traits that demonstrate meaningful differences between groups, around which you can craft strategy.

Let's use our previous example of an automotive mechanic shop. Assume that the business is competent, like most others in the market, but nothing really separates it from the competition. Each has fairly equal access to technology and staff. Should this business launch a mass advertising campaign stating "we're just as good as everyone else"? Obviously that is not a desirable message.

Consider the possible consumer segments that may exist in the market for automotive repair. Perhaps one segment will be interested primarily in convenience (e.g., located close to the customer's home, quick turnaround on their vehicle repairs). A second segment is interested in the highest-quality workmanship. A third segment is interested in a personal touch (e.g., a friendly service representative who remembers your name from past visits, willingness to explain in practical terms the work required on the vehicle).

Certainly, a business like this will probably serve all three segments to some degree and therefore should strive to be convenient, offer good workmanship, and provide a personal touch. But when you invest in your business, it makes sense to focus on making adjustments that would ensure you are a perfect fit with at least one desirable segment.

Market Orientation

Most business owners think of marketing as advertising. Marketing is a more holistic effort than just promotion. It starts with customer orientation. To be specific, the business needs to produce goods or services that customers are willing to purchase.

A marketing-oriented company will first determine what customers require, and then choose which products to offer based on this knowledge. Marketing touches all aspects of the organization when done well. It embraces the concept of competitive advantage. A marketing-oriented company will nurture a culture of excellence around a desired competitive advantage (e.g., if your company strives to nurture a competitive advantage based on workmanship, all employees must embrace this initiative). Systems and processes will be designed that strengthen the company's competitive advantage. Finally, a marketing-oriented company will promote its competitive advantage and focus promotions on the market segment that would appreciate what makes the company unique.

It takes discipline to invest in serving a smaller group of people. And it is also extremely difficult to maintain a competitive advantage over time, because this point of differentiation must remain relevant to consumers in the midst of evolving trends, technology, and consumer preferences.

Everything in this article up to this point involves process. It's a simple formula and is certainly not rocket science. The complexity in effectively marketing your business relates to judgment. Which traits do you use to define market segments? Which customer segment is the most appropriate fit for your company to serve? What internal aspects of your organization do you need to adjust in order to nurture what makes your company unique? What is the primary message that your target market needs to hear to understand how your unique attributes are relevant to them? This judgment is the foundation for good marketing decisions.

Marketing strategy requires trade-offs. Be the best at things that are crucial to your target customer and that make you unique in the marketplace, and do a good job at everything else.

> *If you want to build a ship, don't drum up the men to gather wood, divide the work, and give orders. Instead, teach them to yearn for the vast and endless sea.*
>
> Antoine de Saint-Exupéry

Sales Management

Salespeople are people. These human beings are the same as any other employee in your organization. They perform well when their interests are aligned with those of the broader organization and when a strong leader is able to help them apply their skills and abilities.

Linking Marketing and the Sales Force

Theoretically, marketing and sales should be naturally aligned. Marketing defines many fundamental aspects of your business model, such as selecting a target market, defining the core value you will offer the market, and shaping how that value will be communicated to customers. The sales force management process then organizes salespeople to provide any necessary personal contact and helps facilitate a sale.

Reality is much different. Salespeople often lack a clear understanding of the value their employer is trying to offer. Marketing strategies are often overly complex and have little chance of being implemented because they lack coordination with the sales effort.

Take a close look at how your sales force interacts with your overall marketing effort. Consider how the following concepts would apply to your company.

Explain the Big Picture

A well-functioning sales force is just like any other major system in your business, such as production. For a manufacturing company's production floor to function at peak efficiency and effectiveness, the people involved must understand what they are working toward. They must understand how their actions relate to a broader goal, such as improved quality or reduced material cost. Systems and processes impose controls and direction, but human judgment is often the magic that drives performance.

The sales management system is no different. Salespeople make frontline decisions every day. They represent your company to the customer and choose which points to discuss and which points to avoid. Ultimately, they craft the reputation your company has in the industry and directly affect the volume of products and services produced. Understanding the company's broader objectives allows salespeople to focus effort on products and customers that are crucial to the company's long-term future.

Imagine your salespeople ignoring your new product line because it distracts from traditional technology that is easier to sell. Salespeople may have revenue targets to meet, but no direction or understanding of the importance of this new product to the company. They may have no idea if this product is a passing fad that will not be a priority next year, or if the company is betting its future on this technology and needs to establish a foothold in the market. It is crucial that salespeople understand how their actions relate to the company's long-term vision.

Listen to Your Salespeople

Your salespeople have access to remarkable information. They interact with your competition and customers daily. This information can be valuable in crafting marketing decisions such as setting prices and developing your company's brand image.

Useful data is often overlooked, such as customer feedback on new products. You may have a centralized technical support system in place, but customers will still call their salesperson because of the existing relationship. It would be useful for those in charge of marketing to have some understanding of the number of calls received and the nature of the technical questions that emerge.

Salespeople are busy, and expectations for them to collect information must be realistic. Simplified reporting systems have the best chance of being implemented. Also, it can be useful to reward salespeople for digging up information that has a meaningful impact on future strategic decisions.

Compensate Your Sales Force Properly

Compensation format is a fundamental component of sales force management. It is crucial to design sales force compensation to align with your marketing goals.

Let's return to our previous example of a company involved with a product launch. One of the major decisions will be to determine the selling price. Many companies consider discounting price as a way to inspire consumer demand in the short term. In some situations, focusing the salesperson's effort has a far more dramatic impact on success than lowering the selling price. It may make sense to maintain the original selling price while increasing sales force compensation.

When implementing this approach, provide financial incentives to salespeople for meeting specific goals. For example, certain technical products require salespeople to invest time in educating customers during the launch process. This may reduce the salesperson's compensation during the launch period, because they spend less time promoting traditional products and there may be a delay in sales volumes as customers begin to adopt the new product. One solution can be to provide a bonus or a larger commission on the new product for a short-term introductory period. A bonus helps the salesperson justify spending the additional time on customer education, while also ensuring the product is embraced as a priority.

Support Your Sales Force

Marketing is often responsible for building awareness and ultimately is far removed from the sales effort. Instead, use your marketing effort to enhance the sales effort or to replace steps in the sales process that are a poor use of your salespeople's time.

Some companies have successfully replaced cold calling with sophisticated direct marketing campaigns that can generate qualified leads from a large number of prospects. Seminars can educate clients in a social and credible environment while allowing salespeople to use their client visits more productively. White papers on difficult technical issues can be posted on your website for customer reference and used as a reference tool for salespeople during sales visits or when following up on a sales call.

Agree on What Makes You Unique

Business owners often choose to focus on a niche market. They focus on offering something unique that is important to those customers. Surprisingly, salespeople and marketing staff often disagree on what is important and will promote entirely different benefits. This split confuses the customer and can be detrimental to sales.

Perhaps the salesperson is right and marketing decisions were made without properly understanding the customer. Perhaps marketing is right and salespeople are too focused on what has worked in the past or do not properly understand the unique benefits of the product. Whatever the problem, marketing and sales staff are most effective when they base their decisions on the same information and work together to close a sale.

Any department that operates in isolation rarely makes profitable decisions consistently, and your sales and marketing staff are no different. Tie the sales force closely to the marketing effort and you'll benefit from satisfied customers and a more profitable business.

Motivating Your Salespeople

Whether the sales employees of a private company report to a sales manager or to the owner of the business, someone is responsible for the performance of these employees. Given the significant responsibility of the sales effort in driving revenue and profit, it is wise to consider how best to motivate your salespeople.

Mentor Your People

Everyone, even the most senior salesperson, is continuously learning. Good employees are sponges and soak up information and wisdom that will help them do their jobs.

Sales managers are in fact managers. They must have an aptitude for mentoring employees who report to them. Mentorship can take on many different forms. It might involve coaching the employee, listening empathetically to challenges related to an account, or perhaps simply providing resources that help with skill development.

So what does this mean for strategy? If you are an owner or general manager of the company, you might want to hire a sales manager with those aptitudes. Keep in mind most sales managers are former top-performing salespeople and do not necessarily have the skills needed to manage employees. Many sales managers benefit from leadership and management training.

Provide Clarity

Clarity helps people understand performance expectations. Help your salespeople commit to clearly defined, realistic, and challenging goals.

Clarity of focus starts with the sales management structure itself. For example, the sales manager is responsible for establishing territories and assigning accounts. In some situations, the way that customers are allocated has a direct impact on salesperson behavior and performance.

Consider an equipment manufacturer that sells to large institutional customers as well as small independent companies. We can assume that large institutional customers have a longer buying cycle. The sales manager planning for sales throughout North America might simply allocate territories to salespeople based on geography. But given the differences in buying processes it may be wise to allocate customers based on type, rather than location. Certain salespeople would be focused on institutional accounts, with expectations related to call schedules that fit with long-term sales. Other salespeople would be focused on smaller accounts, with expectations suited to a shorter buying cycle.

Provide Feedback

People perform better when they receive a fair and honest evaluation of their performance in meeting clear goals.

The most effective sales managers have the interpersonal skills to provide feedback constructively. When providing feedback, consider whether your tone is positive. Some salespeople may be skeptical and feel like you are "pumping their tires," but the bottom line is that humans respond well to people who support them. Your salespeople will respect you when you call a spade a spade, but they are more likely to act on that feedback when the message is packaged with genuine support.

It is valuable to provide feedback from the customer, not just the sales manager. I've found customer comments to be extremely useful when the sales manager has less career experience or industry knowledge than the salesperson. Nothing shines a spotlight on performance like direct customer feedback. Feedback must be relevant to be useful, and since every situation is unique you will have to craft a specific set of questions and appropriate method for collecting the information. But as an example, the sales manager might ask a sample of customers to complete a survey critiquing the salesperson on product support, timeliness of responding to customer enquiries, and resolving conflict.

Align Their Interests with Yours

Designing a compensation system is possibly the most complex of all sales management responsibilities.

Salesperson behavior is often difficult to incentivize, and extreme differences can exist between the drivers of short-term transactions and long-term account development. External factors such as swings in the economy can also make previously established sales targets too high or too low.

The key here is to realize performance incentives are a driver of profit rather than an expense to manage and as such deserve careful attention. Performance incentives are effective when they align the salesperson's and the company's goals. One practical way to do this is to calculate commissions based on gross margin. Of course, gross margin is easier to calculate when the company has a sophisticated cost accounting infrastructure. However, in my experience the gross margin calculation only has to be reasonably accurate for salespeople to have confidence in the system. Their behavior is still aligned with company profitability.

Incentive programs may include bonus thresholds to encourage salespeople to achieve difficult goals. These thresholds must be designed in a practical way given the wide range of performance you might see from salespeople with different skills and abilities. Be creative and fair in how you design the program.

For example, part of a salesperson's individual bonus may be based on performance compared with that individual's historical three-year average. A second part of the bonus may be based on common sales goals that apply to every salesperson. This sends the message that everyone is progressing in their career, but also that all salespeople are evaluated against the same standards. Someone who meets a difficult goal will be well rewarded, but someone who clearly hits it out of the park will receive greater rewards.

Hiring and Firing

Building a motivated sales team starts with the hiring process.

Good salespeople have an internal drive to succeed. They want to be financially rewarded, but compensation is secondary to pride in a job well done. Hire people who want to be among the best-performing salespeople on the team.

Of course, not everyone we hire can be exceptional. Sometimes we can accept lower performance, such as with new hires who are just trying to learn the business. But what should you do with chronic underperformers who you know in your heart do not have the skill or ability to meet practical expectations? Recruiting and firing people is one of the most difficult but most important responsibilities of the sales manager.

Beyond internal drive, it is also useful to consider the salesperson's fit within your organization's corporate culture. Will they buy into company values? Will they work with everyone toward a common goal? The natural self-sufficiency that drives success can also make people feel isolated and is a likely reason salespeople love to connect and bond with their peers. This cohesion can help improve overall performance and help people fall in line with company objectives.

Some of these suggestions to motivate salespeople relate to decisions that emerge when developing a comprehensive sales and marketing plan. For example, compensation structure is a core component of sales management. But

some of these suggestions also involve the interaction between the sales manager and employees. In reality, strategy and execution are connected. Motivation is influenced as much by interpersonal relationships as it is by how the
system is structured.

Improving Sales Agent Performance

Rather than being an employee, a sales agent is a person or a company under contract to a manufacturer to sell or distribute products in a given territory. Sales agents can provide significant advantages over employees in certain situations, such as immediate access to markets and a lower level of required supervision.

The relationship between manufacturers and sales agents can be abrasive. Most manufacturers view sales agents as a necessary evil. Few manufacturers feel the sales agents earn their pay or focus on increasing volume.

Sales agents are people. Just like when you're working with sales employees, performance is a result of having the right people on board and forming a working relationship that produces good work. The following are practical leverage points to build a strong sales agent network.

Sales Agencies Are Businesses Too

Just like any company, high-performing sales agencies make money when products can be sold efficiently or when they sell something completely unique. Put yourself in their shoes. What is it like for the agent to sell your company's product?

Is your product easy to move? Sure, you're paying the representative to sell the product and you expect some work for that commission. But you must also realize they'll put their time behind the product in their portfolio with the highest return on investment. Return on investment is influenced by factors such as margin, volume, and how easy the product is to sell.

Does your company offer a high level of sales support and customer service? The sales agent may be responsible for solving customer problems, but rarely can the agent do this on his or her own. Make sure they get information and support from you so they can do their job. The manufacturer and agent relationship often solidifies into a partnership after working through a complex customer problem.

Start with the Right People

Manufacturers generally do a poor job of finding the best agents. They are more focused on finding any agent in a specific region than on finding an agent with appropriate skills and abilities. Before you begin negotiating a representative contract, make sure you're talking to the right potential partner.

To locate sales agents, it can be helpful to interview key customers that will end up buying from the sales agency eventually selected for that territory. Who do they like working with and why? Who would they trust when they need product support? Which sales agencies are complacent and which are hungry to earn that customer's business? When you know who is respected in the region, you will have a greater degree of confidence in negotiating a potential sales agency contract.

When you are interviewing potential agents, ask difficult questions. Does the agent's perception of product support match your company's expectations? Are your agent's expectations of the manufacturer's sales support realistic? Many times the answers to these questions provide clarity on whether there is a fit with your company and the sales agency's corporate culture. Remember, a partnership is like a marriage. Make sure you're selecting the right person.

Support a Quick Transaction

Support your sales agents by enabling them to do their work efficiently. Thirty years ago sales representatives would visit customers on the road from Monday to Thursday and send quotes by mail or fax on Friday. Customers expected up to a seven-day turnaround on a quote. Times have obviously changed with technology.

In many industries, timely and accurate quote information is more important than product quality. Consider what your organization can do to support a fast turnaround. Some manufacturers invest heavily in custom software enabling their agents to spec out products quickly. The customer receives a quote and detailed specifications in minutes. Customers don't have time for best guesses and sales representatives don't have time to make estimating mistakes.

Hold Sales Agents Accountable

Whatever the industry, the worst employees are usually the ones who hate to be held accountable for their actions. They are lazy and often do not pay for themselves. This principle applies to sales agents as well and can manifest in avoidance of tasks such as completing call sheets or providing detailed sales data on their customers.

In my experience, the best sales agents have no problem answering for their actions. No high performers want to be micromanaged, but they also have nothing to hide. The more sophisticated salesperson knows that manufacturers can be easier to work with when they have good data on how their product is sold. This data can help the manufacturer improve factors such as logistics, pricing, product development, and sales support materials.

A common mistake is to simply ignore an agency's performance. Manufacturers may not have time or interest to evaluate and analyze results, and may simply assume that agents are performing effectively. Lack of feedback and follow-up with agents will move your product's priority to the bottom of the pile.

Make sure you understand the nuances in your industry when establishing and developing your sales agent network. Remember, business is about relationships and investing a little time in the people who will influence your success most often pays for itself many times over.

> *Without friends no one would choose to live, though he had all other goods.*
>
> *Aristotle*

Social Media

Business is built on relationships. Social media is just technology applied to how people interact with each other – and with companies. The connections are broader and information is shared differently. But the relevance of social media is rooted in the human need to build relationships.

Connecting Social Media to the Buying Process

In 99.9% of businesses, social media is a new tool in the toolbox. Customers have always connected with each other and shared information about their preferences, trends, and products. Social media tools are ways of connecting that make this interaction quicker, easier, and far more networked among a specific community.

A Basic Definition

Let's establish some definitions as a foundation for this discussion. Online is different than social media. Let's refer to any information available on the Internet as online resources. That might include resources as diverse as product reviews conducted by an independent organization to a company's own webpage showcasing its product.

Social media is a collection of social network sites where members can share information and build relationships. Often, when using the term social media people are referring to a community that is connected online. Twitter, for example, allows people who sign up to receive posted information from a select number of other Twitter members. Hundreds of these different social network sites exist (Twitter, Facebook, LinkedIn, etc.), each with its own culture, usefulness, and distinct sub-communities. Some social network sites allow pre-existing networks of people (e.g., high school friends) to interact in new ways given the technological benefits of the Internet. Other social network sites introduce people to new people, based on a member's personal interests. As a result, these social network sites can provide strong bonds among their communities of members.

To keep things simple, social media marketing can be defined as the process of interacting with members of social media sites for the purpose of drawing attention to your company or product. This usually involves creating content (e.g., an article or video) and encouraging people to share it with their networks. Although the interpersonal dynamics are different, there is some parallel to the way consumers share information in person through word of mouth.

How Does Social Media Influence Purchases?

There are two parts to this answer. First, we have to understand the customer's buying process for the product or service we are talking about. Second, we have to understand how a specific social media site works.

An Evolving Customer Buying Process

When examining the customer buying process, consider the stages at which customers seek out information. In some industries, these buying processes are evolving as consumers gain access to new information through the Internet.

The automotive industry is a great example. Fifteen years ago a car buyer would stop by several dealerships to learn about different vehicles, and then stop by at least one dealership to negotiate a purchase. Today, customers spend several hours researching different vehicles online, and walk into one or maybe two dealerships to have a few final questions answered and take a specific vehicle for a test drive. This holds true for a 66-year-old grandmother as much as for a 16-year-old high school kid.

The implications for an automotive dealership's sales process are tremendous. Salespeople still have a crucial role, but customers want them to play a different role. Customers still need the same knowledge about a vehicle, but they want to get it online rather than from the salesperson. People look to automotive manufacturers' websites and online product reviews for information, but they also share opinions among their communities.

There are also implications for an automotive dealership's marketing process. Customers are now more likely to seek information on a vehicle online rather than relying on traditional media such as newspapers or radio. Many segments are still influenced by these forms of promotion, but nearly all customers will research their options online before walking into a dealership.

Let's step back from this example for a minute. The tendency for people to seek out opinions from their peer group has always been part of a customer's purchase process. If we consider an industrial example, twenty years ago the owner of a machine shop that required a new lathe would speak to a few sales representatives, develop a short list of options, and likely phone some other machine shops that operate the same equipment to get their feedback on issues such as quality and performance. Now, that same process happens but the machine shop owner is able to use Google to develop a wider set of product options on the short list. The peer conversations are happening online through discussion forums, with the chance for a greater number of people to provide input.

The major shift in a customer's buying process is largely due to the fact that anyone can post information at any time on the Internet. There is so much information available that customers no longer have to rely on an expert, such as a sales rep who has a deep technical understanding of the equipment.

The trend manifests in how people make decisions in their daily lives. People trust authorities less and rely on their personal networks for information. The recent trend away from child immunizations is a perfect example. Rather than trusting the opinion of the established medical community, many young parents are relying on opinions found in Facebook posts and comments by Hollywood celebrities.

Here is the key point. Consumers rely more on their social networks for information than in the past, and they access those networks in new ways. This information shapes people's behavior.

Each Social Media Site Is Used Differently

Each social media site can be considered a different tool. Just as there are differences between a reciprocating saw and a table saw, each site is useful for completely different situations.

You need to understand how some of these tools are used, and specifically whether they have implications for your customers' buying process. But there are hundreds of different social media sites available, all with their own subtleties in how they are used. The following is meant only to provide a few concise examples of how people use the three main social media sites.

People use Facebook to connect with personal friends, many of whom are long-lasting relationships from many years ago. Many Facebook users value personal relationships and are genuinely interested in the lives of the people they connect with. Using Facebook, however, also provides a venue for people to express themselves as they post information about their own lives. That helps people define who they are, and when people are in this mindset they often feel comfortable connecting with lifestyle-oriented companies. Facebook is a good venue to connect with a small, tight community that shares opinions about products. For example, a gluten-free restaurant might develop quite a strong following on this social media site.

LinkedIn is essentially a database of contacts that people make through their work careers. But some people use LinkedIn far more than this, posting information about their professional lives or following certain companies that are relevant to their professional interests. Many people use this social media site to introduce themselves to new customers, suppliers, and peers.

Twitter is used to learn more about specific people (e.g., politicians, friends, or thought leaders) and special interest topics (e.g., fluid dynamics). People post information that other users of the site can read. People use the site to build their own networks, share what is happening in their lives, and seek out education.

As a high-level summary, the primary reasons companies engage with people on social media sites are to meet new potential customers, create a new touch point for contact (often where valuable content can be distributed), and build brand awareness.

Using Social Media Effectively

If your customers are going online for some of their information related to your product or service, you have the responsibility to ask yourself how you can be part of that process. I'm not saying that social media is the right answer. But it is prudent to ask the question.

Using social media effectively is incredibly difficult. A customer will seek out information silently from fellow consumers and also from potential suppliers. Businesses have many different options to provide information online, but in most situations it is extremely unlikely that a potential customer will find that information. At most, your potential customer may use only one or two social networking sites for the purpose of researching your product, and you may not have access to your potential customer's personal online network. The odds are stacked against you.

Social media as a tool is evolving and becoming a more important part of how people purchase most products and services. We need to learn as marketers. That does not mean we should be wasteful in our marketing expenditures. Rather, we should be careful about how we spend on social media, learn from what does not work, and build on the successes.

Let the Conversation Evolve

One challenge we face as marketers is that we do not control social media the same way we control traditional advertising. We're used to controlling our message, such as when we place an advertisement in a newspaper.

Let's say our company manufactures specialized software to help engineers design airplanes. It's probably fair to say that engineers deeply involved in the aircraft design process are a relatively small and tight-knit community. We can assume that many of the people in this community share common interests related to work, and we have the opportunity to provide some useful information to them through social media sites such as LinkedIn or Twitter. One option may be to post an article or a video outlining some aspect of our software and share it through these sites.

In this example, what would we do if a person in that community watches our video and then comments that the software is ineffective? What recourse do we have? Many business owners are scared of interactions they do not control. That's just part of the medium. Many people choose to ignore the odd negative comment (or reply to it directly, promptly, and respectfully) but are prepared to react to a crisis. There are different opinions on how to handle such situations, but the main point is that they will occur. Social media involves, after all, a discussion rather than a monologue.

Here's the point. Effective use of social media stems from customers engaging in dialogue. Your promotions need to draw people into a conversation. Whether they simply forward someone else's content or share their opinions, engagement is the goal.

Developing Good Content

Deciding how to connect with people through social media is very difficult. But once you understand how, the real magic happens when you create useful information for your potential customers. This is referred to as content.

The content you create must be directly relevant to your customer and be presented in an interesting way. That takes deep knowledge of who your customers are, what information they need, and what will appeal to them. It takes left- and right-brain skills. Developing good content that customers find useful is extremely difficult.

I have found three core questions to be highly valuable. First, what information do customers need? As a potential supplier, consider the questions your customers most often ask. Understand the information they are seeking out.

Second, where do customers get information? Just referring to the Internet is too broad. Consider whether they gravitate to customer-review websites, read articles and white papers on a topic, or seek information from their friends' posts on Facebook.

Third, what content-based promotions can we create to get customers the information they need? The social media strategy will likely embody general awareness-building as well. But our goal should be to draw them to us in the purchase process. Tailor the promotions in a way that encourages people to interact, whether sharing the content with others or commenting on it.

There are many different types of content, each of which is well suited to a specific industry or company. Video is becoming extremely popular in many situations because it is so entertaining as a rich visual experience. White papers (basically, opinion papers a few pages long) can give valuable background to customers entering a purchase process. Infographics are usually highly visual one-page descriptions of a complex process or a few key pieces of information. There are many options, and they are constantly evolving.

Keep in mind that customers usually do not have a shortage of content. What makes your company's content useful? Relevance. Embrace the principle that narrow is better and prepare content for a niche market. Don't just produce a video on the top ten questions people ask when buying a new home. Focus the topic on the top ten questions that newlyweds ask when buying their first home. People are interested in content that is relevant to them.

Distributing Content

You essentially have two ways to distribute your content. You can use a push or pull strategy.

A push strategy sends content out to people. In the realm of social media, this generally means you send a message or post content that is presented to a list of people who have chosen to connect with you through a social media site.

Push strategies can be highly effective. Some people have a large number of Twitter followers who are deeply interested in their opinions and the content they post. For example, an industrial robotic equipment manufacturer, Yaskawa Motoman Robotics, based in Ohio (@Yaskawa_Motoman), posts a variety of content on Twitter relating to robotics use. It has thousands of followers who are interested in keeping up to date with this information.

A pull strategy posts useful content that functions as a magnet to draw potential customers into your company's sales process. This is difficult. The trick is that customers must be aware of the content. It's a bit like setting up an information booth at the side of the road and hoping potential customers happen to stop by.

The strategy usually requires an exceptionally effective job of search engine optimization (SEO), which is ensuring search engines such as Google can direct people to your content. The process also involves posting the content where your customers can access it. Your own website is an obvious choice, but not all customers seek out useful information from their suppliers' websites. Many customers search for information on YouTube or on consumer review sites. Or, in some cases, they rely heavily on content distributed by their friends on sites such as Facebook and Twitter. Each situation is different. You need to know where your customers go for information and find creative ways for customers to engage with you.

If you own a retail store that sells running gear, your Facebook site likely will have information that builds the brand relating to an active lifestyle. You might post information on new products or recipes for healthy meals. If you offer free information (e.g., a downloadable article on preparing for your first marathon) to people who Like your page, this could be considered a pull tactic because you are creating an opportunity for customers to engage with your company. There are several variations to this qualifying-step tactic of Liking or Following your company on a social media site, such as offering electronic coupons or entering the person's name in a contest.

Advertising on Social Media

In addition to posting useful content, companies like yours can pay to advertise on social media websites. But companies often lack clarity on how to advertise on social media. One reason is that advertising options on the social media sites are constantly evolving.

Banner ads were the popular form of advertising online in the early days, but now they are generally perceived to be less effective and several other options now exist. Each of these can be tailored to your marketing objectives, and many times the cost is directly related to measurable results. Twitter, for example, allows you to choose an objective for a specific advertising campaign. Your objective may be to engage with more people (e.g., you pay for your ad when people re-tweet information you sent out), to direct people to your website (e.g., you pay when people click on your tweet to be directed to your website), or to generate leads (e.g., you pay when a customer sends you their email address to get information on a product).

Although the cost of advertising on social media is generally based on results, it can be frustrating and confusing to price these advertising campaigns. Most social media sites use a bidding system to price their ads. You can set parameters such as the maximum you'll pay for someone to click through to your website, or the maximum per day you'll spend on the campaign. But the process is different than traditional advertising and takes some practical use to understand how to use it effectively for your own business.

Like all other forms of advertising, clarity improves results. Know what you want to achieve from your social media advertising campaign. Then you can choose your budget and tailor your message accordingly.

Integrating Social Media with the Sales Force

Customers are more in control of the information flow than a decade ago. They share information with each other and choose where they get information. They do extensive research before contacting the salesperson. However, our sales management structures are set up for the old way of interacting with customers.

There are a few possible changes companies can make to improve the effectiveness of their sales force in the face of these changes.

Adjust the Salesperson's Role

In some situations, it makes sense for the salesperson to adapt to the customer's new buying process. Customers are often far along the purchase process before the salesperson gets involved. This reduces opportunities to present alternative solutions that may be a better fit for the customer or could improve company profitability.

One option is for the salesperson to play a deeper and more involved role. It may make sense to step in at an earlier stage of the buying process. With industries where salespeople are used to being the first stop in the buying process, that means getting out of your building and connecting with customers before they are deeply engaged in the sales cycle. This type of change can be awkward because it involves salespeople changing how they operate. Many times salespeople are used to dealing only with hot incoming leads, and stepping in at earlier stages of the purchase process can involve more rejection and greater effort for less direct gain. Some situations may actually call for an entirely different salesperson with a pre-sales role who simply connects with customers before they are ready to buy. There are many sales force management considerations for this situation, from salesperson profiling (it may require salespeople with different skills or different personality types) to a different compensation structure.

Adapting the sales process can take more radical adjustments. It may be necessary to shift from a consultative to a transactional sales approach. Clearly, this needs to be accompanied by a proactive effort to connect with customers in other ways before they begin the transaction, such as presenting background information online to draw customers into the sales cycle with your company. Another variation would be to adjust the interaction between the new-business sales effort and the after-sale customer service effort.

Content Should Support the Sales Effort

Chances are good that customers now seek out information online that used to be supplied by your salespeople. That's the starting point for the type of content you can consider producing for your customers. But when considering how to integrate this with the sales effort, consider where you can insert the salesperson into the customer's buying process.

As an example, let's imagine you have a company that manufactures custom-made protective cases for sensitive diagnostic equipment that must be transported in hazardous environments. A protective case such as this may be necessary in the presence of flammable gasses, vapors, or dust. Traditionally, salespeople have provided technical support and helped customers define specifications early in the process. Although all products are custom made, customers are now attempting to learn about their options online before contacting a salesperson. There is a risk that your potential customer will connect with a different supplier before your salesperson enters the conversation.

In this situation, consider tying the salesperson to the technical information that the customer is seeking online. One way to do this is to give enough information in the online content to catch the customer's interest and establish your company as having expertise relevant to the customer's search. At that point, the salesperson is mentioned as being able to provide custom information relevant to each customer's situation. This approach can work well if the salesperson is presented as a resource. But some companies stumble and present the process of making contact with the salesperson as a barrier. It feels to the customer like they have to reveal themselves to get any useful information at all. That unfortunate situation will likely steer good potential customers away from the salesperson.

Another approach is to make the salesperson part of the content. If the customer won't go to the salesperson, take your salesperson to the customer. In situations where salespeople have a technical and consultative sales role, there is potential to present a salesperson's knowledge and opinions in your online content.

It is important to understand how customers engage with certain types of content at different stages of the buying process. Infographics, blogs, and articles provide quick information that can introduce many different people to your company and not all will be potential customers. White papers and webinars provide more in-depth information, and people who invest time in learning from these resources are typically deeper into the buying process. Case studies and customer testimonials are historically used by salespeople, but may be useful to post online for people to learn from as they finalize their education process and prepare to engage with salespeople.

Integrate the salesperson into the content used in later stages of the buying process. Videos of a salesperson reviewing the features and benefits of equipment may fit nicely with this approach. White papers or articles authored by the salesperson can also be effective. It is useful to present the salesperson front and center as the authority on the issue because the salesperson then gains credibility with the customer. When the customer needs additional information, it is a natural next step to contact the salesperson.

In addition to introducing the salesperson to the customer, content can be a valuable resource for the salesperson to use in a sales meeting. The reality is that most potential customers that contact salespeople will not have seen all the content your company posts online. A resource such as a white paper can be a useful background document for salespeople to provide as a leave-behind after a first meeting with a potential customer.

Salespeople Can Listen Too

When a company has an active social media strategy, it is possible that customers are engaged and there is some dialogue going on between customers about the company or even directly with the company itself. This may be in the form of posts to a social media site such as the company's Facebook page, but it may also be in the form of a blog external to the company somewhere on the Internet.

The company employee looking after creating online content is probably not a salesperson. Usually, that responsibility is allocated to someone with a different skill set. If this is the case, that employee is likely the most in tune with these customer dialogues. Specific topics that may emerge include the concerns that people raise, the compliments they make about the company or product, and the unmet needs that customers discuss when chatting amongst themselves.

Clearly, there is an opportunity for salespeople to listen to and learn from these public and open conversations. At the very least there is value in having a summary of these relevant customer insights presented to salespeople for their education and to spur discussions around possible follow-up with specific customers or leads.

All of the suggestions above involve some aspect of culture change among the sales force. Salespeople are notoriously averse to change of any kind. This is particularly true when the proposal is inspired by a technological innovation. But when a company's employees realize that their sales structure is outdated, they tend to see the benefits of adapting to the situation.

> *You have to learn the rules of the game. And then you have to play better than anyone else.*
>
> *Albert Einstein*

Frontline Decisions

Strategy that has any reasonable chance of success must be firmly rooted in reality. For this to happen, the big-picture strategic direction must be tied to daily decisions such as how to price a product or structure promotional campaigns. To make good frontline decisions, we must understand what works in the world of marketing.

Creativity Can Sell

Have you ever watched an interesting television commercial and one minute later forgotten what was being sold?

Creativity used effectively in advertising is more than artwork. It is a tool for breaking through advertising clutter and educating your potential customers on your product. However, for creativity to be effective as a selling tool, some core principles must be followed.

Have a Purpose

The graphic design studio or advertising agency you are using will need to know who your target market is and what you want to tell these potential customers. As basic as this may be, most businesses at some time have used advertising that presents the wrong message or focuses on the wrong audience.

Here is a basic example. Perhaps you wish to promote your recreational vehicle dealership's wide selection of used RVs to young families who have the potential to enjoy an RV lifestyle for the first time. Without this information, the graphic designer will need to rely on his or her own past experience with RVs to develop the ad. You may very well end up with an ad targeting senior citizens who are current RV owners and wish to upgrade to a new luxury model. This would not help your dealership sell more used RVs. A little direction goes a long way.

Walk in Your Customer's Shoes

It doesn't matter if you find your own company's advertisements interesting. If you are selling clothing to teenagers, you obviously need to understand the nuances in teen culture that affect what they find interesting. Develop advertisements that appeal to your customer, not yourself.

Effective graphic designers think like the people for whom they're designing advertisements. They walk a mile in this target market's shoes before they develop a creative approach. The designer should know what motivates this person to make a purchase. What reason do customers have to use the product? How do they feel about the purchase? How do they feel about peers watching them use the product? These three issues vary in importance with different industries but they should all be considered when determining what will help make a product appealing to a customer.

In our RV example, perhaps the primary motivation of first-time RV owners is to enjoy family time and to revisit their own childhood memories of camping. The emotional aspect of how first-time RV owners feel about their purchase is a strong foundation on which to build an appealing creative message. You need to understand the customer to sell to the customer.

Tie in Your Key Message

The tricky step where most advertising fails is in the actual use of the creative idea.

Your creative concept must drive home the reason people would buy from you. It must do more than get the attention of your audience. It must reinforce what makes you unique.

Years ago I saw a television ad promoting Saturn cars. A young woman calmly approached a salesperson and explained she had lost her job and was no longer able to purchase her new car. The sales rep was supportive in his response. The next scene showed the same woman walking into the dealership again and proudly explaining she was now ready to purchase her car. The sales representative just smiled in a way that said, "I knew you could do it." This commercial did a fantastic job of illustrating Saturn's unique sales experience, one of the company's core benefits.

When planning your advertising, consider how you can make your ad more effective. A slightly different twist on a traditional message may be helpful if it catches the attention of your audience and drives home your message in a memorable way.

Setting Your Price

Of all the difficult decisions in business, one of the most complex is setting the final price for a product or service. There are many possible approaches to the task, from a rigid mathematical analysis to gut instinct. No wonder people tend to just match their competitors' selling price or increase their own selling price from last year by an arbitrary percentage.

There is a better way. It is simple, logical, and easy to implement. Take the time to understand the floor and ceiling for your potential price, and then use a combination of your creativity and instinct to appeal to your target customer.

Understand the Floor: Your Costs

The floor is the lowest price you can charge without losing money. This is your cost to produce the product. Without getting lost in the complex world of cost accounting, I find that most entrepreneurs with a non-financial background have an easier time of working with a floor price that includes two things:

- **Variable costs:** The incremental costs you incur to produce your product, such as labor and materials.
- **Fixed costs:** The overhead to run your business, such as your own salary and your power bill.

Here is a simple example to illustrate the point. Let's assume you have just started a new company and are manufacturing specialized electronic testing equipment for the mining industry. It costs you $25,000 in labor and materials to manufacture one of your units, so your variable cost per unit is $25,000. You expect to incur $500,000 in overhead expenses this year and expect to sell 100 units, so your fixed costs per unit will be $5,000. It's simple math: your floor is therefore $30,000 per unit ($25,000 in variable costs plus $5,000 of overhead per unit produced).

The above example is meant to be a generalization. For example, the number of units you sell will likely be influenced by the price you charge. A higher price may mean you sell fewer units, which raises your fixed costs per unit. Also, this floor does not include a reasonable base expectation for company net income. The process is organic, and at this stage we just need a practical estimate to work with.

The principle here is that you have to know what your costs are in order to charge a price that ensures you make money. Get your costs right and you'll have a true understanding of your floor.

Understand the Ceiling: What Your Customer is Willing to Pay

Depending on your industry, estimating what your customer is willing to pay can be far more difficult than estimating your costs. It requires an understanding of how your customers think and of the competitive options in the marketplace.

The key here is to understand how the customer perceives the value you offer, relative to your competitors. The decision is often heavily influenced by emotion, whether you are selling to consumers or to other businesses. In our previous example of selling equipment to mines, the engineers who procure equipment are likely risk-averse. As much as their structured procurement process is rigid and focused on ensuring a fair or even lower price than market average, there is usually no incentive to those employees for trying out an unproven supplier.

For the sake of our example, let's say your competitors provide similar equipment for $60,000 per unit. Let's assume that your ceiling is $60,000.

Creativity and Instinct

The distance between the floor and ceiling prices provides you with a pricing window. The next step is to consider what options you have within this window and select a price point based on its fit with your broader sales and marketing strategy.

We have to consider the different groups of customers, or market segments, that may emerge as potential customers. Each may follow different steps when making a purchase and be motivated by different factors. As a result, each will likely have a different price ceiling.

With our mining example, competitive pressure is a significant issue to consider. Mine employees often view multinational suppliers as safe and local startup suppliers as higher risk. It is not likely that a mine will switch suppliers simply because of price, but if it does take on a smaller supplier it is likely that the mine management would expect a lower price. There may not be a rule of thumb here, but in this situation let's assume that mine management expects your price to be roughly 10% less than an existing supplier's, so roughly $54,000.

Consider that $54,000 to be a reference point for your strategy, not a final determination. Your product's features and benefits relative to the competing product are relevant to setting a price. You may be able to charge a higher price than this reference point if your product is more durable or if it has enhanced functionality. But then again, maybe the best you can hope for is that the mine would try your product given its points of differentiation, but still expect the 10% discount.

Continue to be creative in this step. Would the mine be open to an entirely different pricing structure? For example, you could offer a monthly rental price for the equipment, which would essentially package equipment with ongoing service and support while guaranteeing that the equipment will be operational over the life of the rental contract. This may be perceived as a lower-risk option, but it may also have other benefits, such as moving the transaction from the mine's capital equipment budget to an entirely different maintenance, repair, and operation budget.

Every industry and company finds itself in a unique situation, and the more time we can spend in our customers' shoes the more likely we are to select a pricing strategy that is practical and effective.

Creative Pricing

When setting a price, you can adopt simple tactics that work in other industries. Remember, every industry has its own nuances, and not every tactic will work for your company. Take what fits and modify it to your situation.

Give Price a Voice

A high price says that your product is better than a competitor's product. Imagine you must choose between two brands of glue to repair your broken antique china teapot, one priced at $10 and the other at $12. The value of the teapot far outweighs the $2 price difference. If the teapot is important, you will pay 20% more for the possibility of better glue.

If you cannot charge a premium, make price silent by charging the same price as your competitor. Customers focus on price when they cannot tell the difference between two products. If you are negotiating with a customer, protect your gross margin and offer concessions on less-costly variables such as delivery time.

Increase Quantity

Selling a higher volume often has a dramatic impact on gross margin. Service companies often find small and large jobs result in similar costs. In the banking industry, the transaction cost of providing a $5,000 loan is nearly identical to that of a $50,000 loan. Some manufacturers can almost double their price for twice the volume with only a minor increase in production cost.

For this to work, quantity must be important to your customer. In the teapot example, selling 16 oz. for $15 and 3 oz. for $10 may not increase your total sales revenue. Most people do not repair fine china often, and they would have no need for the larger bottle.

Package Your Price

Salespeople often introduce a premium product and then show the mid-market option. The customer references everything against the premium product, and chances are they will spend more than they planned.

Imagine shopping for a mountain bike. The salesperson first shows you the most expensive bike in the store. You will now compare every other bike against what you truly want, and most likely upgrade your purchase. There are many ways to package your price. Telephone companies bundle local phone service, high-speed Internet and long distance. Bundling works in part because it takes the customer's eye off the individual price of each service.

Customers are happy with a slight discount and the convenience of a one-stop shop. Tiered pricing is also commonly used. Charge a basic price for a basic product and higher prices for a product with a clearly defined additional benefit. For example, some airlines increase prices as a flight date approaches. Consumers are willing to pay higher prices for the convenience of a short-notice flight.

Use Wasted Capacity

Work you can schedule during traditional downtime is like found money. The key is to price the work properly. Imagine a manufacturing facility that shuts down Fridays in July because orders are traditionally slow. Use this time to schedule lower-priced work. Assuming your overhead is accounted for through regular sales, this additional production only needs to be priced higher than variable costs. Be careful when using this strategy. Will your core customers be offended that they do not receive the same discounted price? This approach works best when selling to a different region or a different customer base.

Selective Discounting

Everybody loves a deal. For many industries, sales promotions that discount price, such as coupons, can move inventory, generate short-term profits, and introduce your product to new customers. But if you sell a premium product, protect the integrity of your brand by providing a different benefit (e.g., free furniture cleaner with every kitchen table purchased) rather than discounting the price.

In the long term, price discounting can also work well when used as a tool to strengthen relationships. A high-end men's clothing store that holds a special sale exclusively for existing clients is saying thank you to the people who purchased in the past year.

Getting your foot in the door can be difficult. Companies that rely on long-term customer relationships, such as software companies that require future product upgrades, often initially set a discounted price and retain customers through non-price factors such as reliability and exceptional service.

Drastic Discounting

Offering a drastically reduced price with a "door crasher" feel to the promotion is one of the most effective pricing tactics used today. Most often a true discount strategy involves presenting the lower price as a deep discount and also providing a clear reason why such a low price is being offered. For example, clearance sales to move old stock or limited-time sales to celebrate seasonal holidays are commonly used methods of justifying drastic discounted prices.

The scope of the discount that is required to significantly increase demand depends on your company's situation. Some industries never discount prices and any decrease is perceived as a deep discount. However, other industries, such as clothing and vehicles, require a significant reduction in price to capture the attention of consumers. The key here is that the consumer will reference the discount against what they feel is an alternative purchase situation.

As with any tactic, discount pricing should be used appropriately for each situation. Companies can face problems when they permanently offer deep discounts. Many retailers have built their entire business around a segment of the market that is addicted to artificially low prices. It can be very difficult to charge appropriate margins regularly when customers are constantly watching for the next big sale.

Odd-Number Pricing

Pricing a product at $29.99 rather than $30 is certainly a gimmick, but it can work in some situations when selling to consumers. Many times when customers view price as a crucial factor in their purchase decision, they will view an odd number used in the price as a special deal. Intellectually, people realize the company simply chose this number as the sale price. But subconsciously people seem to gravitate away from round numbers.

When to Charge for Extras

Most owner-managed businesses intentionally allow hidden value to creep into their customer experience. By not charging for every little thing, such as rush orders, international shipping, and training, they offer something small that means a lot to the customer. The trick is to realize which free extras are beneficial. If these extras are not important to your customers, recapture lost gross margin by adding these costs to your price. However, if your customer recognizes the value and you need to distance your company from competitors, be generous. New customers may be willing to pay a premium for your standard service if you offer a complimentary benefit, such as free shipping.

Few business owners think through their prices. Paralyzed by indecision, companies often simply adopt industry standard prices and hope for the best. Take the time to consider how simple changes to product pricing can influence the way your customers buy.

> *Leading in a complex world means recognizing the simple things you can do to make things better.*
>
> Condoleezza Rice

Unique Economic Situations

When the operating environment changes for better or worse, pressure builds to adjust around opportunities and challenges. Difficult decisions must be made in times of uncertainty. Clarity often comes from focusing on business fundamentals such as the needs of the customer and the basic drivers behind the health of your company.

Battling a Weak Economy: Selling to Consumers

When an economy softens or even declines, consumer confidence crashes and purchasing habits begin to change. Marketing strategy must respect structural shifts in consumer behavior, such as the factors that motivate purchase decisions and the steps in a customer's purchase process. The following are a few practical ways companies can adjust their approach to marketing and sales.

Adjust Your Advertising

The customers you are targeting dictate the places you choose to advertise and the message you use. What they want from you may be different when the economy is soft. People get scared for their safety, which may influence the steps they take when they make a purchase or the traits they look for in the product itself. Automobiles are a good example of this. In an uncertain economy, we could expect many consumers to seek out fuel-efficient options, lower-priced vehicles, and more reliable brands.

If only consumers were so predictable. Human beings also wish to reward themselves, and their purchase decisions are not so logical. When times are difficult, people often want to escape the stress. They reward themselves with impulse or luxury purchases. This may involve picking up a carton of premium ice cream from the grocery store – or splurging on a new vehicle. The general trend may be toward restraint and conservative buying behavior. But we also have to appeal to the emotional side of the purchase decision.

You will need to adjust your advertising strategy around consumer behavior in your specific industry. Changing your message to suit the needs of your customers is half the equation. But if your customers now get their news information from different sources or spend their time in different places, you may also need to shift where you choose to advertise.

Manage Your Price

When consumers face difficult times, obviously they become more sensitive to price. In many cases price becomes more important in their purchase decision. But with some segments of your market, chances are good that people focus on value rather than price. Examine the value you are providing for the price you charge relative to your competitors' products. Your loyal customers may begin to price shop rather than just reorder. Be one step ahead of the process.

If you feel you are not providing adequate value, consider a price cut. If you feel the value you offer is high, maintain your existing price and communicate the features and benefits people receive for their money.

Pricing is complex because it involves more than a number on a sticker. There are aspects to a customer's cost other than price that can build value into what you offer. Payment terms are one example, as many customers would prefer to buy on credit when the economy softens. If your business is in a position to offer credit to your customers, you might offer financing or rental options. You may be surprised at the increased profitability of a rental arrangement compared with a traditional purchase.

In a tight economy, some customers avoid any additional costs, such as a warranty. But more savvy customers examine the total cost of ownership and may find tremendous value in options that require additional fees. For example, a customer who purchases a new furnace for their home may seriously consider extended warranty programs or subscribing to an annual service contract.

Expect Behavior Changes

Customers often take more time to make decisions when they are in a difficult financial position, simply because the purchase is more important to their financial situation. Expect people to need additional information they did not require before. They may ask for discounts or shop around to a few other suppliers to prove to themselves they have selected the right option for their unique situation. It can be frustrating, but if you want to do business in this environment you have to adapt your sales and marketing process. Get them the information they need. Make sure your salespeople expect these delays and are patient and informative when required.

Changes may materialize in how people spend their time as well. Most families will still take a holiday. But they may select a location closer to home or seek out a value-priced option. People's perception of risk changes in difficult financial times, and they begin to prefer the safety and security of a stable home life. Rather than taking that dream holiday to Disneyland, they may choose a completely different option, such as buying a new pool table for their home.

Changing Your Product

Consider altering your product or service offering to fit with price-sensitive customers. For example, if you own a retail tire service dealership, you may choose to offer two options for switching over winter tires. A higher-priced service could be offered for scheduled appointments, and a lower price may be offered to customers willing to leave their vehicle for a 24-hour period.

Your change may be to how you present the product rather than to the product itself. People really do judge a book by its cover, and it is important to use attractive and convenient forms of packaging. But there are often several options, and it can be possible to lower your product costs significantly by considering alternative suppliers or new packaging.

Avoid making changes for the sake of providing something new. The point behind any product decision is to focus on what customers want and need.

Battling a Weak Economy: Selling to Businesses

As consumer spending declines, your customers and vendors will have less money to spend. Companies will change how they do business and how they plan for the future. Business relationships will change, creating opportunities for growth and improving profitability. Consider how you can work with the factors in your industry that are under your control.

Revamp Your Marketing Strategy

When an economy softens, all aspects of the marketing strategy that got you to this point should be open to revision. This includes something as fundamental as your company's product line. In a strong market, a manufacturer can be too busy filling orders to realize that one of its product lines actually loses money. Revisions may also be required to keep operations efficient and lean. Necessary changes might require laying off staff or adjusting processes.

A completely different aspect of a marketing plan that often requires attention when the economy softens is the company's distribution channel. When times are tough, people may change where they shop. If you are a food processor and have focused on specialty food retailers, consider how consumers may reduce luxury purchases and seek out value in mainstream grocery chains. Which sales agents, distributors, or retailers will connect with your target market?

Cost pressure has forced some manufacturers to bypass regional distributors and sell directly to the retailer. In some industrial situations the manufacturer can bypass local sales agents or dealers and sell directly to the end user. This strategy is obviously destructive to the established distribution network. In many industries, intermediaries may fight back when omitted from this direct approach. However, many manufacturers are forced to use an alternative route to the customer to preserve their profits.

Consider fixing problem areas outside of your marketing plan during a slower phase. A high-growth economy can cause serious problems such as underperforming employees or unnecessary overhead. Now is the time to replace underperforming staff, shave unnecessary expenses, and rethink how you organized and operated your business in the last few years.

Focus on Important Relationships

When examining the health and relevance of their business relationships, most entrepreneurs wisely focus on relationships that are working well. Your key suppliers, distributors, and customers face uncertainty. Now is the time to shore up your relationships with these companies. Let them know your company is prepared to roll with the punches. Tell them you intend to maintain open communication and support their business. This can pay off in the short term, as businesses will begin to refocus on key partners. In the long term, they will remember who was willing to support them through tough times. Actions speak louder than words. For example, if one of your suppliers is clearly having difficulty, offer to pay your account sooner than required. Strengthening key relationships pays dividends.

Once your key relationships are safe and secure, examine the other relationships in your business. For example, evaluate your broader customer base and consider where your profit is generated. Over time the nature of each customer's business will evolve and of course profitability will change as well. Consider what each customer truly values and make adjustments to improve profitability by cutting unnecessary features or adjusting the working relationship. Then replace the remaining unprofitable customers with ones that are willing to pay your price. That final step often involves some difficult choices and at times is not at all easy to implement. But it is important to maintain the profitability of your business. This exercise may require a significant change in other areas of your business. A proper analysis of your customers will often point to an underperforming product line or regional office. Deal with it.

Buy Competitors and Pursue New Industry Partners

Strong revenue hides bad decisions. Companies that lack efficiency will likely face financial problems as revenue drops. Capital will be more difficult to access, and companies in trouble may have their loans called in by banks. Watch for competitors that begin to lay off sales representatives, hold deep-discount pricing promotions to clear out inventory, and generally behave abnormally. These competitors will make mistakes, and their relationships with customers will deteriorate.

As companies become weak or fail, the industry channel will reorganize itself. That means there may be opportunities to buy poorly managed companies that nonetheless have valuable physical assets and talented employees. Opportunities occasionally emerge to form partnerships with a failed company's traditional vendors.

If a weak economy triggers a period of consolidation, consider how it affects your operating environment. Your suppliers may become larger and gain more negotiating power. Your local competitors may be purchased by a multinational with a more aggressive business philosophy and deeper resources. The operating environment will change.

Manage Your Balance Sheet

Keep a strong balance sheet during tough times. With limited funds to lend, banks will focus on the highest-quality business clients. If you do need financing, you want to be a favorable candidate with strong cash flow, high-quality receivables, and inventory liquidity.

If credit tightens, consider selling your receivables to a factoring company for a small fee of a few percent of invoice value. Your benefit is cash in the bank instead of uncertain receivables.

A strong balance sheet can be a competitive advantage. Financing expansion will obviously become more difficult for everyone. That's a good thing if you are better financed than your competition. If your competitor's hands are tied, you may have an open market to pursue.

Leveraging a Strong Economy

When an economy exits a period of decline or stagnation, consumers and businesses breathe a sigh of relief. Everything gets easier and a company's focus can shift in an improving economy to a comfortable growth tempo. You may see signs that a normal economy is returning, such as qualified labor becoming a bit more difficult to find. But the real difference is attitude. Consumers and businesses are cautious but positive. Companies focus on regrouping and reorganizing their businesses.

There is a difference between an improving economy and a high-growth economy. High growth is like drinking from a fire hose. Skyrocketing revenues and thick margins hide operational errors and poor decisions resulting from tight timelines. Businesses are not operating efficiently, and customers unfortunately get used to poor customer service.

The following are a few important considerations as you prepare your marketing and sales effort to handle growth, whether the economy is in its early stage of improvement or entering a period of rapid expansion.

Predict the Future

It is extremely difficult to get ahead of a market. It takes a keen eye to see where a market is going and entrepreneurial instinct to understand how your company can position itself to capitalize on the change. But it is necessary in a growing economy to have this vision.

From my experience, the best we can hope for is to patch together a combination of hard facts and anecdotal evidence. An example of hard facts is the value of building permits as an indicator of construction activity six to twelve months from now. An example of anecdotal evidence is whether commercial real estate agents see increased inquiries from local business owners considering expansion.

Be Patient

As an economy begins to grow, put yourself in a position to serve your business customers. Ramping up for growth takes time. Your potential customers will be considering vendors as they prepare to spend money on inventory, expansion into new product lines, and expansion of their facilities. Knock on their doors now, and be ready when they choose to expand operations.

If the current growth phase was preceded by a period of difficulty, not all of your customers will be in a position to take advantage of growth. Economic devastation is selective. Some companies will have been hit hard while others may have had no problems at all. Some consumers will have been laid off while others feel secure in their jobs. Understand how your customer base was affected and adjust your strategy accordingly. For example, if your business customers are short on inventory, offer a restocking promotion. Partnerships built in hard times often lead into strong business relationships that last for many years.

It pays to remember that cash is king. That goes for your customers' businesses as well. All businesses and consumers wrestle with cash flow, no matter the economic situation. Recognize the importance of flexibility when establishing how your customers will pay your bill. This is a period of change. People are reconsidering their vendors. Adjust your terms to help your customers.

Expect Less Room for Error

If the economy is improving but not yet firing on all cylinders, there is still precious little room for making mistakes. But in growth mode, mistakes will inevitably happen. The point is to take calculated risks and try your best to avoid the worst-case scenarios that may emerge. It's now time to properly plan and make careful decisions.

There are benefits to diversification, not least of which is the ability to spread risk across multiple sources of revenue. However, expansion into new markets or new products involves some level of risk as you deal with the unknown. When expanding in a growing economy, it usually pays to stick to your knitting. Build on your strengths but don't diversify into areas that are beyond your ability or are simply too risky. Depending on your balance sheet, this may not be the time to absorb the financial repercussions of a bad decision. For most businesses, a growing economy is a good time to build on current expertise and ramp up operations related to what your company does best.

Operate Profitably

The mature and seasoned entrepreneur knows the importance of operating profitably, but only because he or she has previously made the mistake of ignoring profit. It happens to everyone. When a company finds itself in an extremely busy period, the entrepreneur focuses on revenue rather than profit. The thought is that once we ramp up revenues we can always make adjustments to become more profitable. Wrong. Something will occur, like the economy slowing down (it always does eventually). Run your business with the objective of making a profit every day.

When an economy takes off, excitement builds. Competitors are scaling up and aggressively pursuing new business. Customers are ready to spend money. Be careful to avoid the crowd mentality. Question everything. Is the industry really as busy as it seems? Are customers really becoming less sensitive to price? Does it really make sense to double production capacity?

Think over the longer term when working with customers you know will be around when the economy returns to a normal tempo. They may expect slightly higher prices today, but be careful not to take advantage of the situation. Make sure you maintain customer service levels for these core customers. They have long memories. The way they are treated in busy times will influence their purchase behavior during slower periods.

Expect your systems and processes to break during periods of growth. Predict how the future will unfold. Ask yourself what will occur if your company experiences a 20% increase in sales orders. Will salespeople be able to enter the necessary data into the order system? Will your inventory levels be adequate? Can you maintain service expectations for delivery and after-sale service? These systems and processes affect customer satisfaction, but also profitability. Data errors, stock-outs, and product deficiencies cost money. Deal with them before they occur.

Focus on Drivers of Growth and Profit

Every company has a small handful of core activities that drive growth, and a few others that drive profitability. Sometimes the same activity will drive growth and profit. But because industries and companies are unique, expect the activities important in your business to be different from what matters to a company in a different industry, or even from those activities important to your direct competitors.

Here is an example. If your company manufactures agriculture machinery, chances are high that it sells through a dealer network. Your direct competitor may have a well-developed dealer network in place, whereas you may be in the early stages of locating and securing dealers. Clearly, the health of a dealer network in this industry is important to growth and profitability. But these two competing companies will be involved in very different activities. The mature business may need to focus on helping existing dealers expand market share within their territory, whereas your company may need to focus on identifying, evaluating, securing, and training new dealers.

> *Growing up, I was taught that a man has to defend his family. When the wolf is trying to get in, you gotta stand in the doorway.*
>
> B.B. King

Family Business

When a family owns a business, relationships add complexity to owner-ship and management decisions, but also strengthen the competitive nature of the organization. Family bonds can create an unquestioned trust between family members. Decisions can be made with a long-term view that spans multiple generations. A deeply personal culture often permeates the organization, tying family and non-family members together. The business is the family. The family is the business. This produces intense passion and commitment.

Improving Performance in the Family Business

When considering how to improve the performance of a family business, it is natural to focus on the interpersonal relationships among family members. These relationships are what make a family business unique. However, the true opportunity to dramatically improve performance in a family business often rests in how business strategy is created and implemented given the family dynamic.

As the direction of the company is established, corporate goals are set that influence decisions such as selecting the industries in which the company will compete and the products and services the company will offer.

It is absolutely crucial to acknowledge and fully understand the family goals that influence these strategic decisions because they influence the direction and financial performance of the business.

Balancing Corporate and Family Goals

The family dynamic has an impact on high-level corporate strategy, not just the company's culture and management style. For example, some of the most important strategic decisions that a business owner can make are influenced by the desire to build the family legacy. Despite the possibility for higher financial returns, risky growth strategies might be discouraged because failure may tarnish a respected family name in the business community. There may also be pressure to maintain family control, with the intent to ensure future generations have the opportunity to continue in the business.

Family goals are varied in nature. The same family business might value providing a rich and rewarding management training experience for an upcoming generation, as well as protecting wealth as a method of financing the exiting generation's retirement. Other family goals may be entirely personal, such as increasing local employment as a way of giving back to the community.

As these examples illustrate, family goals are often inherently interrelated with corporate goals such as target financial returns and the company's mandate for growth. Whenever possible, family goals must be balanced with consideration for factors that influence corporate direction, such as the level of risk that the business will take on and desired market share.

The Succession Plan and Corporate Strategy

A succession plan involves more than the transfer of equity. It involves transferring the management of the business to a new generation of owners who must make complex business decisions.

The nuts-and-bolts process of preparing a business plan or strategic marketing plan can ensure the business addresses the issues of the day while helping prepare the business to operate without the exiting generation. These results are accomplished when two generations work together to develop strategies to drive long-term growth. If both generations collaborate in this planning process, both will feel ownership of the plan's direction and genuinely view this next phase as a natural step in the historical growth of the business.

The process creates a venue to ask sensitive questions, such as these:

- **Who should take over the business?** Will this selection be made in the family's best interest (e.g., maintain the family legacy) or the company's best interest (e.g., promote the most competent person, whether they are a family member or not)?
- **What is the appropriate equity structure?** Should the outgoing CEO draw as much personal wealth from the business as possible or leave equity in the business to provide stability? Should debt or an equity partner be taken on to facilitate the exit?

Engaging multiple generations in a strategic planning process also encourages diversification. Entrepreneurs flourish when they are personally interested in the industry in which they operate. Their interest enables them to see trends and understand nuances in consumer preferences, resulting in good business decisions. It is common for family businesses to diversify as younger generations are provided with greater authority over corporate strategy, begin to select which industries to enter, and define how the business will be structured to compete within those industries. A healthy family business will embrace new opportunities for growth.

A Patient War Chest

Marketing and finance are tied, as a cash reserve is often required to generate growth. One of the primary benefits to many family businesses is that a war chest may exist after decades of profitable operations.

A growth plan developed for a business with access to capital that thinks in the time frame of generations has the benefit of tremendous flexibility. For example, a family business may be more likely to invest in high-quality equipment that provides lower operating costs (therefore establishing a competitive advantage), with the view that the premium price tag can be amortized over many years.

A structured approach to planning can improve the performance of a family business by aligning corporate and family goals and ensuring that marketing decisions within the organization respect the unique characteristics of the family enterprise.

Strategic Decision-Making in a Family Business

For a family business to be successful, it must embrace what makes it unique. This principle rings true in many facets of the business, such as determining which staff to hire and how to finance the business. It is also a fundamental consideration for how strategy is developed. The strategic planning process should work with this unique DNA, not against it.

As a simple definition for our purpose, strategy involves making decisions on the long-term future of the company. Strategic planning is focused largely on the future of the company as a whole. What type of business will we be in based on matching the strengths of our business to market opportunities? Business planning and marketing planning build from decisions in the strategic plan and establish an overall blueprint for what the company will attempt to achieve and how. So what is unique about how family businesses approach strategy?

How Decisions Are Made

Decisions in family-run organizations are made differently from decisions in non-family organizations. It is important to accommodate the unique process that many family businesses use when making decisions.

In a traditional corporate structure, the company's CEO and management team (i.e., employees) will create a long-term plan and take this to the board of directors (i.e., people representing the company's owners) for input and approval. In a family business, the CEO is likely a parent who essentially has authority to develop and approve the long-term plan. That parent may choose to bypass senior managers and seek input from the children working in the business. There's nothing wrong with involving these future leaders of the company early in their careers. But we should also realize that senior managers in the family business often bring a great deal of insight to strategic alternatives. These senior managers may feel isolated when excluded from the process. Many times when I'm working with a family business we choose to involve the management team to draw in this perspective. Each situation is unique and these subtleties should be considered.

Family businesses have a great ability to adapt to the market environment and pivot quickly, compared with the multinationals they often compete with. This maneuverability allows family businesses to be flexible and adapt to market conditions. Preserving this shortened decision-making process can be a source of competitive advantage.

One complaint I often hear is that some family businesses (particularly the founders, who are often less process-oriented) will seem to make flippant decisions and operate without any strategy in place at all. In most situations, the opposite is true. Most of these entrepreneurs tend to have a long-term vision and a plan for how to get there, but they have not placed this plan on paper and shared it with others in the organization. There certainly are benefits to a more formal process. The quality of decisions improves when the entrepreneur's assumptions are challenged and the strategy is fleshed out with an additional level of detail. As well, sharing the plan with management helps these key employees ensure their actions are aligned with long-term priorities.

One of the greatest strengths of family businesses is inherent patience. Decisions often take into account the impact on children or grandchildren. This mutigenerational view changes the planning horizon from perhaps five years to decades when making decisions related to investment or building competitive advantage.

Differing Priorities

Owners of family businesses generally treat their companies as tools to achieve their personal goals. Therefore, strategic decisions are made in the context of what is in the best interest of the owner rather than the company.

A family business with multiple owners can face conflicting company priorities. For example, a retiring generation may be focused on removing equity from the company while younger family members may be in growth mode and wish to invest company profits in new ventures. Acknowledging and considering each family member's priorities can help resolve conflict and ensure the company direction is acceptable to all family members.

Factors Unique to Family Business

When I'm helping family business members with strategic or marketing planning, we also have to address special considerations inherent to their situation.

The dynamic among family members is often different from that among employees. You usually can't fire family members, the love-hate relationships can be intense, and there are inherent power issues between family members. The result is an interesting chemistry in the senior management team and it affects the planning and decision-making process. When conflict does exist, the family members must put personal differences aside and contribute to developing a plan for the company. If not, it is unlikely that a plan will be in place and the company will operate like a rudderless ship.

Multi-generational businesses are proud of their family legacy. In fact, nurturing and protecting this legacy is in some cases more important than the financial success of the business itself. There can be tremendous pressure on younger generations to protect the family reputation and the family's standing in the business community. People may begin to avoid risk, which runs opposite to the entrepreneurial spirit that drove the company's founder. The impact on company strategy is tremendous, given that strategy involves making choices, such as which products to offer, which markets to enter, and which customers to serve based on risk-versus-reward judgment calls.

Exiting the business can also be difficult. Most families would not be comfortable selling the family business if the new and unrelated owner could operate under the family name. When preparing a marketing plan, conscious decisions must be made on how closely to tie the family identity to the company brand.

Success in a family business often requires embracing the very traits that set it apart from non-family enterprises. Building around the decision-making processes, the owner's priorities, and the factors that make the company unique will help ensure the process used is appropriate and the final game plan is practical enough to be implemented.

Branding During Ownership Succession

Your brand is your company's reputation. For many companies, the owner's personal identity is a significant component of the company brand. Managing the owner's public profile during succession has a direct impact on your company brand.

Founders often have magnetic personalities, and the company's reputation may be built on decades of the founder's public exposure. The founder is the business. Care must be taken to adjust the company's reputation so the business will not only benefit from the credibility and history of the founder, but also reflect the additional depth and substance of the broader organization.

Adjusting a company's brand image is a fundamental component of a strategic marketing plan and must be carefully managed over a period of time. It is best not to tackle this task the day the founder leaves the business.

In most situations, it is useful to distance the exiting owner's reputation from the company's brand. Each company is unique, so the process must be approached in a customized manner. The following are considerations that may influence your company's brand strategy during ownership succession.

Pick a New Spokesperson

The incoming spokesperson is usually from the next generation of ownership. Of course the new owner must have the personality to represent the company in order to pull this off. And there may be some troubles down the road when this new person leaves the business and the same problem is sure to arise again.

One alternative that is appropriate in some situations is to avoid a single spokesperson and instead place several key employees in the public eye. These people can be rotated based on the nature of the advertisement or public message that must be presented. As long as a consistent impression is left with the public (e.g., these are quality people who stand behind the product) this approach is highly flexible and can work extremely well.

Leverage the Family

The family reputation itself can be a source of credibility and a powerful component of the company's brand image. When appropriate, a family identity (not just the identity of one family member) can serve as a foundational plank on which the company's brand is built.

Companies associated with a prominent family are likely to be associated with local ownership, which many customers interpret as trustworthy and oriented toward customer service. Also, family business philanthropic activities help develop a genuine connection with the local community. The community becomes part of company values and culture, which permeates the brand.

When a prominent family member leaves the business, it may be appropriate to enhance the business's connection to the family rather than just one incoming family member taking on a leadership role. The family brand can have strengths beyond those of a single person and longevity beyond the career of the incoming generation.

Keep in mind that in many cases the exiting family member will have left a significant mark in the community. For reasons of maintaining the company culture as well as enhancing the external company brand, family businesses often celebrate the role that previous generations played in serving the business.

Transfer Key Relationships

We most often consider a company's brand to be a relationship between the company and a mass market. But it is useful to also consider relationships with certain people. When managing your company's brand image, transfer the owner's relationships with key business contacts to others within the company.

As an example, a company's distribution agreement with a key supplier may simply dissolve once the founder leaves the business because it was based on a handshake deal twenty years ago. In a situation like this, it's crucial to phase the new leadership (son, daughter, or key manager) into that relationship. Business is based on trust, and people must trust the company once their primary contact leaves.

A second example involves a key customer. It is natural for key customers to question whether they should seek out other suppliers once their long-term friend gets out of the business. Customers usually have multiple contacts with alternative suppliers, and this is a rare opportunity for your competitors to steal your business. If you protect the relationship, you are protecting the company's brand.

A third example can be found in a company's connection to its industry. Many times a founder will serve on the board of an industry association or a local business association. The company's new leadership may choose to take over this responsibility and continue to build relationships in these organizations to ensure the company maintains its profile and benefits from this window of insight into industry developments.

Keep the Same Message

Consistency builds credibility. If the company was promoting timely delivery as its primary competitive advantage before the founder left the business, then continue this message after the founder steps back from the spotlight. This consistent message will help consumers and suppliers feel they can continue to trust the company after the leadership change.

Promote the Business in New Ways

In some situations, it is appropriate to take the focus off the founder leaving and instead put the emphasis on the company itself.

Essentially, we are packaging the removal of the traditional spokesperson with the launch of an entirely new method of promoting the business. For example, a company could launch a new advertising campaign that promotes the company's traditional message (e.g., timely delivery) but in a new and creative manner. This campaign may not in fact use a spokesperson at all. People may or may not notice that the spokesperson is missing from the ads, but if the creative campaign is high quality, the message will still resonate with the audience.

Respect the Previous Generation

Lack of respect for the outgoing generation is rarely a problem, but it emerges occasionally when an extremely young and inexperienced person is handed the keys to the business. He or she naturally wants to put a unique stamp on the company and may not have the track record to understand the history of decisions made in the past. Also, sons and daughters tend to have a deep understanding of their parents' faults but are less likely to grasp the true value of the parents' strengths.

Beyond the fact that it is the right thing to do, there is a business case for showing respect to the outgoing generation. Customers and suppliers will usually have good relationships with the outgoing leadership and therefore be most comfortable with a leadership transition when this person is given an appropriate level of respect for how they have run the business.

The Departing Owner Must Buy In

People will read the departing owner like an open book. The owner will convey a feeling of confidence if he or she is comfortable with the successor's ability. Clearly, people will take this signal as a guide to form their own impression of the incoming leadership.

The easiest way to build genuine confidence in the incoming leadership is to work at it over time. Create a situation where the next generation would be given greater decision-making responsibility over the course of several years. The reason is simple. It takes time for someone to learn how to make good senior-level decisions. It also takes time for the existing owner to feel comfortable with the younger generation's ability. A successful track record of good decisions is needed.

The pinnacle of this process is reached when both generations are sitting at the same table making joint decisions in the business. This is particularly true when a founder's children take over the company. The parent usually has final say on the decisions by virtue of the familial relationship, but once the two generations can see each other as peers, the owner can more easily step back from the spotlight.

The personal dynamic between incoming and outgoing leadership in any organization can be complex. It is even more complicated in family businesses. However, it is worth the effort to build the necessary level of trust. A relaxed and orderly departure in which the outgoing owner clearly supports the incoming leadership will have a positive impact on the company's brand image.

Conclusion: Tying It All Together

Marketing touches nearly every aspect of an organization, not just traditional areas such as product development, pricing, branding, and customer service. Marketing decisions connect directly to so many other areas of business. For example, focusing on selling customized product may require Operations to restructure its production floor. Rebranding is almost always tied to a change in corporate culture. And the launch of a new product will require deep coordination with Finance, given the impact on expenses and revenue.

So as a business owner, what is your role in the sales and marketing effort? You are the architect who puts forth a vision for what is possible. You are the craftsman who uses skill, sweat, and experience to create something from nothing. And you are the symphony conductor responsible for maximizing the talent within your organization to produce something unexpected, impressive, and perfectly suited for the audience you serve.

I am grateful you have taken the time to read *Pursuing Growth*. May it help you create value in the eyes of your customers.

About the Author

Brent Banda is a marketing strategy consultant and has worked closely with almost two hundred companies over the last two decades.

The situations where Brent is most likely to become involved include launching new products, entering new markets, and refocusing a company's current marketing and sales plan. These periods of change build value in a company and drive profit.

Brent holds an MBA and has taught as an assistant professor at St. Francis Xavier University in areas such as advertising, professional sales, and marketing management.

For more information visit www.bandagroup.com.

Share your own story!

I have made the chapters in this book available to a select list of business owners for some time. People are constantly sending me stories about the positive impact of this information on the growth of their businesses. I'd love to hear from you as well.

Has this information helped you think differently about your own business? Has your business grown as a result of changes inspired by what you have read in these pages? If one of the concepts in this book relates to your personal situation, here's your chance to share your story. Visit www.pursuinggrowth.com and send me a message.

Also, I'd appreciate hearing your suggestions for topics you would like to learn more about. Your idea might be the genesis for a new book!

Brent Banda

Pursuing Growth *is available for purchase from the author at www.pursuinggrowth.com and from major book retailers. Special discounts are provided when multiple copies are purchased for purposes such as corporate gifts, sales promotions, fundraising, or education.*

Sign up for Brent Banda's e-newsletter and receive additional marketing tips for free throughout the year. Visit www.pursuinggrowth.com.